D0276509

HORRIBLE HISTORIES

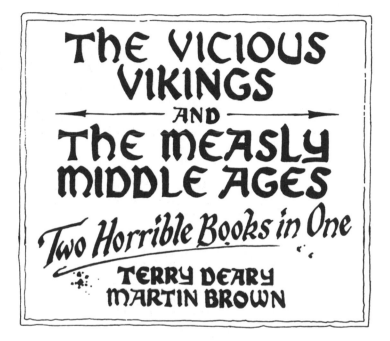

THE VICIOUS VIKINGS

— AND —

THE MEASLY MIDDLE AGES

Two Horrible Books in One

TERRY DEARY
MARTIN BROWN

■ SCHOLASTIC

Scholastic Children's Books,
Commonwealth House, 1-19 New Oxford Street,
London WC1A 1NU, UK

A division of Scholastic Ltd
London ~ New York ~ Toronto ~ Sydney ~ Auckland
Mexico City ~ New Delhi ~ Hong Kong

Published in this edition by Scholastic Ltd, 1998
Cover illustration copyright © Martin Brown, 1998

The Vicious Vikings
First published in the UK by Scholastic Ltd, 1994
Text copyright © Terry Deary, 1994
Illustrations copyright © Martin Brown, 1994

The Measly Middle Ages
First published in the UK by Scholastic Ltd, 1996
Text copyright © Terry Deary, 1996
Illustrations copyright © Martin Brown, 1996

ISBN 0 590 54364 4

Printed by WSOY, Finland

2 4 6 8 10 9 7 5 3 1

The right of Terry Deary and Martin Brown to be identified as the author and
illustrator of this work respectively has been asserted by them in accordance with
the Copyright, Designs and Patents Act, 1988.

Contents

The Vicious Vikings

The Measly Middle Ages

THE VICIOUS
VIKINGS

This book is for my Aunt Molly
Simply the best

INTRODUCTION

History is Horrible. Far too horrible for adults to learn about. You see, people change as they get older. They get "civilised" . . . that means "soft". Now young people, they enjoy a bit of horror . . .

They love a bit of pain and suffering . . . as long as the sufferer is a teacher or the nasty grown-up next door who keeps your ball when it goes over the fence!

But adults try to protect poor children from horror stories. They put labels on films that say, "Not suitable for children". And they don't tell the whole truth about history.

So here's a chance for pupil power to strike back! Here is the *truth* about the Vikings. The things that teacher never tells you because teacher's too chicken-livered. Now you can watch Miss faint in fright as you describe some vicious Viking inventions . . . for torture! See Sir swoon as you explain how Sigurd was killed . . . by a *dead man!*

This book is not suitable for adults. They will say things like, "Yeuch!" and "How sick!" And, when they do, just look sad and say, "It's true. But that's horrible history!"

VICIOUS VIKING INVADERS

The Vikings lived in Scandinavia – that's the posh word for Sweden, Denmark and Norway. The Saxons lived in England – they'd moved in when the Romans left.

All of a sudden, the Vikings started raiding Saxon England! And they weren't very nice about it. In fact they were pretty vicious! Lots of clever teachers will try to tell you why the Vikings suddenly crossed the cold North Sea and raided the suffering Saxons. But do they really know?

WANTED

Job: Pillagers. Brave, loyal men to work overseas
Qualifications: Must be ready and willing for adventure but not afraid to die
Hours: Long and hard (but a lot of excitement is to be had – would you rather stay at home and starve ?)
Pay: Plunder-the more you steal the bigger your share. If you are lucky you could even end up in the Viking heaven of Valhalla !
Special note: This is an urgent vacancy -sailing tomorrow
Extra-special note: This post is not for the fainthearted
     Apply within

VISIT THE SUNNY SAXON SHORES

FREE!

- Longboat Holidays present a **four-day** hit-and-run excursion for the **high-spirited** and **adventurous**. A must for the young and the young at heart.
- **Don't miss** this golden opportunity to **invade** the British Isles. You can **never** call yourself a true **Viking warrior** until you have taken part in the plunder, slaughter and violence of this once-in-a-lifetime experience. A chance to acquire **slaves, riches** and Christian **souvenirs**.
- Pick-up point: the mouth of the **Limford** on the west coast of Denmark. Travel up the coastline — navigation will be by means of a plumb-line, where water depth allows. We will then proceed to open sea using knowledge of **seabirds**, wave formations and the position of **sun** and **stars**. With good conditions we will reach the north coast of England within **36 hours**.
- This holiday of a lifetime is absolutely **FREE!**

What would a Viking want in England?

Work? Or adventure? What were the real reasons for the Viking invasions? Teachers and historians *should* be able to tell you, of course . . . but can they? Which of the following reasons do teachers and historians give for the Viking raids?

1 It was getting too *crowded* in Scandinavia – the Vikings wanted more land

2 The monasteries were an easy way to *get rich quick* on treasure and slaves

3 There was *too little food* in Scandinavia because the soil was useless – it hadn't been kept fertile with fertiliser because the Vikings didn't know about such things

4 There was *too much food* being grown in Scandinavia – the Vikings needed to trade some of it

5 Viking rules meant that younger sons got *no land* when their father died – they had to go overseas and pinch someone else's land

11

6 Some pretty *vicious kings* took over in 9th-century Scandinavia – many Vikings sailed off to escape from them

7 A change in climate made Scandinavia *cold and uncomfortable* – even wild, wet England was better than that

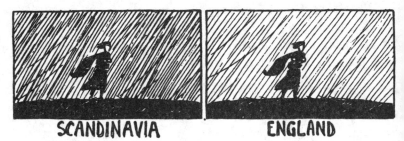

SCANDINAVIA   ENGLAND

8 There was a sudden *shortage of herring* in the North Sea – their main food supply

9 Sea trade was growing in the north of Europe – more trade meant more chances for *piracy* . . . Viking piracy!

10 The Vikings *enjoyed sailing and fighting* better than staying home and farming

> **Answer:** *All* of them! Historians have argued each one of these reasons at some time or another. They can't all be right. The truth is no one *really* knows why the Vikings began raiding.
>
> (It's a bit like the dozens of reasons given for the disappearance of the dinosaurs – lots of clever ideas . . . no real proof!) In the end you have to make up your own mind.

The fact remains, the Vikings arrived. This is how it happened . . .

VICIOUS VIKING TIMELINE

AD

787 Three boatloads of Vikings land on Dorset coast. A Saxon tax officer orders them to appear before the Saxon king. The Vikings kill him. Perhaps they only came to trade.

793 Whirlwinds, comets and fiery dragons seen in the sky over northern England. Bad signs. Sure enough, the first Viking attack on Lindisfarne Priory follows. Monks taken as slaves or thrown in the sea. Vikings go home for the winter.

851 Vikings stay for the winter in England for the first time.

865 Vikings make first demand for Danegeld – in other words, "Pay us lots of money or we'll do nasty things to you!"

870 Vikings discover Iceland.

871 Alfred becomes King of Wessex. He batters the Vikings at Eddington. He rules the south and lets the Viking Danes rule the north of England.

878 Alfred defeats the Danish King Guthrum – they make peace.

886 Treaty of Chippenham divides England into two parts – Danelaw in the north – England in the south.

899 Alfred dies.

982 Erik the Red discovers Greenland.

986 Viking Bjarni spots America but doesn't land.

1000 Leif Erikson lands in America.

1013 Svein Forkbeard threatens to attack England. Ethelred, the English King, pays him off.

1017 Svein used the money to make an even bigger army. Svein dies and Viking Canute (Knut to his friends) becomes king of all of England.

14

1030 Christianity becomes religion for most of Norway after centuries of worshipping the gods of Norse legends.

1048 As if Viking attacks aren't enough, Derby and Worcester are hit by the worst earthquake in living memory.

1066 Viking Harald the Ruthless attacks York. English king Harold Godwinsson defeats him. But William of Normandy lands on the south coast of England. Harold Godwinsson rushes to meet him. William defeats Harold. Normans rule – end of the Viking age.

VICIOUS VIKING LEGENDS

You may think the stories you heard as a child were vicious – *Jack and the Beanstalk*, for example, where the poor old giant bashes his brains on the ground.

Or *Red Riding Hood*, where the wolf gobbles Granny before she pops out again when the woodcutter lops its head off.

Or that poor old witch in *Hansel and Gretel* who gets pushed into her own oven – all she wanted to do was eat the grotty little boy who'd been chomping her chocolate and nibbling her nougat.

But vicious Viking legends are even more disgusting! Viking story-tellers used to recite long poems, *sagas*, that told of disgusting deeds and horrible happenings.

Gruesome gods and shocking sagas

If you believe the poets who wrote the sagas then you'll believe the following . . .

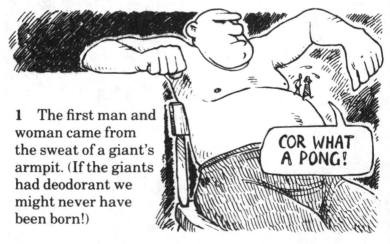

1 The first man and woman came from the sweat of a giant's armpit. (If the giants had deodorant we might never have been born!)

COR WHAT A PONG!

2 There was a huge flood in the early days of the world – just like Noah's flood in the Bible. But in the Viking story the flood was the blood of a dying Frost Giant. (Maybe that's why there's a Red Sea!)

3 Those aren't clouds you can see in the sky – they are the brains of a dead giant!

HE MUST HAVE BEEN A DIM GIANT

4 The sky is held up by four dwarves called North, South, East and West. You'd better hope their arms don't get tired!

5 If you die peacefully then you go to Hel. And Hel – unlike Hell – is very cold! If you want to go to Heaven then you'd better die in battle.

6 Some people were born to be slaves – the *thrall* class of people. They were ugly, stupid and clumsy but strong. The first thrall family had charming girls with names like Blob-nose, Oaf, Dumpy, Fat-thighs, Noisy, Servant and Bundle-of-Rags. The brothers were called Cattle-man, Hunch-backed, Ashen-face, Horse-fly, Shouter, Clott, Drott and Stinking. (And you have the nerve to complain because your parents called you Wayne or Deborah!)

BLOB-NOSE   OAF   DUMPY   DEBORAH   FAT THIGHS

7 *You* might not believe in giant gods who rule the world but the Vikings did. Odin was the god of magic and war, poetry and wisdom. If you wanted him on your side then you'd have to make a sacrifice to him. At one sacrifice ceremony a traveller reported seeing dead dogs, horses and humans hanging from trees. There were over 70 bodies hanging side by side.

8 Statues of the god, Frey, usually showed him with no clothes on. When a Christian bishop saw one he was so shocked he took a hammer and smashed it.

9 Heroes who died went to a heaven called Valhalla. There, they fought all day and drank all night. If they were killed in a heavenly battle they came back to life in time to fight the next day. When they feasted they drank from the skulls of their enemies.

10 The Vikings converted to Christianity around the year 960 AD after a priest called Poppo performed a miracle. He held a red-hot piece of iron in his hand without burning himself. He said this proved Jesus was greater than all the Viking gods. King Harald agreed and became a Christian there and then.

In your childhood stories, the goodies always won. Cinderella lived happily ever after because she was sweet and kind. But in vicious Viking stories the *cruellest* usually won! And the craftiest! If the Vikings had told the Cinderella story then the Ugly Sisters would have married Prince Charming . . . then murdered him and lived happily ever after in his palace. Cinderella would be one dead duck.

That's the sort of story the Vikings liked as they supped their mead and listened to the poets. And poets were very, very important people, as this story shows . . .

Blood, spit and tears

"Spit in this jar," the great god, Odin, ordered.

"Why should I?" the god, Thor, grumbled. He had a hammer and went around hitting people who argued with the gods.

"Don't argue, Thor, just do it," Odin sighed. It would take too long to explain to thick Thor just what he was up to. "Look," he said, holding the jar under Thor's nose. "All the other gods have had a spit."

"Cor!" Thor said thoughtfully . . . or Thor-tfully. "What you going to do with that lot, Odin?"

"Make a man," the chief god said.

"Oh, well, here goes," the hammer-horror shrugged and spat into the bowl.

TPUPPP

SPLOT!

And, using his great and godly magic, Odin made a man. He called him Kvasir and sent him down to Midgard – Earth.

Now Kvasir was the wisest man on Earth. (So would you be if you'd been made from the spit of gods.) He solved lots of problems for the people of Midgard.

Everybody loved Kvasir. Well, nearly everybody. There were two brothers, Fjalar and Galar, who absolutely hated him! Now Fjalar and Galar were mean, nasty and jealous of Kvasir. So would you be if you were a dwarf who lived underground with hundreds of other smelly dwarves. And Fjalar and Galar were dwarves.

"It is said that the blood of Kvasir is magical," Fjalar muttered one dark day . . . underground, all the days are dark.

"Is it?" Galar asked.

"It is. And we are going to get his blood," Fjalar chuckled.

"We are?"

"We are. Now this is the plan . . ."

"The plan?"

"We invite Kvasir to a party here . . ."

"A party?"

"Yes, you know, a booze-up. And when he's good and drunk you stab him!"

"You stab him?"

"No, *you* stab him," Fjalar hissed.

"What'll *you* be doing while *I* stab him?" Galar asked.

"I'll be waiting with those jars to catch the blood. Right?"

"Right!"

So the dastardly dwarves carried out their plot and bled Kvasir drier than a smoked pork pie.

The dreadful duo mixed the blood with honey and made it into honey wine – mead. And whoever drank the mead would become a poet and a wise man.

The trouble was, no one got to drink the mead. The bloodthirsty brothers kept it to themselves.

And as the years passed they grew crueller and crueller. One day they entertained the giant Gilling and his wife.

"He eats a lot," Fjalar grumbled.

"A lot," the gruesome Galar agreed.

"Let's get rid of him!"

"Get rid of him?"

"I say, Gilling," Fjalar cried. "How about some fresh sea air. It's getting stuffy in here! How about a sail in our boat?"

"Good idea," Giant Gilling growled. "You coming, Mrs Gilling?"

"You go, dear," Mrs Gilling grumbled. "I just get sea-sick. Have fun!"

But Giant Gilling had no fun. The deadly dwarves sailed out to sea and tipped him overboard.

"I can't s . . . glug-glug-glug . . . wim . . . glug-glug . . . specially with this stone round my . . . glug . . . neck! . . . glug-glug . . . I'm going to . . . glug!"

21

"And that's the end of him!" Fjalar chuckled.

"And her?"

"We'll break the news. Perhaps she'll buzz off home," the devious dwarf muttered.

But Mrs Gilling didn't go. She just sat there and cried.

The giant tears fell on the floor and sloshed around the cave. "Me feet are sopping wet!" Fjalar fumed.

"Mine too."

"So get a large millstone and stand outside the cave," he told his brother. "When she steps out through the door just drop it on her head!"

Galar hurried to obey and Fjalar spoke to snivelling widow Gilling. "Just step outside and see the sea. I'll show you where your darling husband met his watery end . . . that's right . . . just step this way . . . no, after you. Right, Galar, drop it!"

Crunch!

"Cor! Stone the crows! It worked!" the brothers cheered. They went back to their cave and slept a happy sleep, until . . .

"Knock! Knock!"

"Who's there?"

"I'm Giant Sattung Gilling – looking for my mum and dad."

The giant boy was huge and wild and very, *very* angry.

"Your dad got drowned," wee Fjalar whimpered.

"With a great big millstone," gormless Galar grunted.

Sattung grabbed the two dwarves by the collar. "You tied a millstone around Dad's neck and threw him in the sea?"

The two dwarves tried to answer, give some explanation. But it's hard to talk when giant fingers wrap themselves around your neck.

Sattung marched into the sea. He walked for miles until the water almost came up to his chin. He dumped the dwarves down on a tiny rock. "The tide is out," he roared. "And when it rises up again you'll have to swim back home!"

"It's much too far!" fat Fjalar sobbed.

"Well, then, you'll have to drown . . . and serves you right," the giant orphan said and waded back to land.

So Fjalar and his stupid brother lost the mead of poetry.

And *no one* . . . not Kvasir, Giant Gilling, Mrs Gilling, Gilling Junior or the dwarves . . . lived happily ever after. What a lovely story!

Vicious Viking myths

Myths, sagas and tales of the supernatural were common in Viking times. People believed that dwarves, giants and evil monsters were in constant battle with the gods. Stories ranged from the creation of the world, to its end, or *ragnarok*. Imagine a world in danger from demons and monsters, who at any time could create chaos and disorder!

Forget your warm and cosy houses, your televisions and computers. Gather round a blazing open fire, shut out the cold winter's night. It's story time – Nordic style.

Government Health Warning: These stories are gruesome – if you suffer from nightmares then don't read them in the dark – you'll strain your eyes for a start!

Bedtime story no. 1

Once upon a time there was a god called Loki. Loki was an evil god who caused a lot of trouble amongst the other gods. He was an absolute nuisance (just like your brother or sister); very jealous and spiteful. Such was his cheek that he once wagered his head in a bet with Brokk the dwarf.

Loki lost the bet, but to save his life he pointed out that there had been no mention of his neck in the bet. Brokk couldn't take Loki's head without harming that neck!

Knowing just how bad-tempered dwarves could be, Loki should have known better than to cheat them. But they got their revenge. How? By sewing his lips together! Moral of the tale: if you want to shut the school bully up – get the help of a dwarf.

But the story doesn't end there. This little incident did not stop the mischievous Loki. He gave blind Hod (the son of chief god, Odin) a piece of mistletoe to poison him. Hod, unable to see, took the mistletoe and died.

But the gods decided to punish Loki forever, so they tied him to a tree trunk and left him there.

Bedtime story no. 2

Thor was the god of strength and hard work. He was also the god of storms. People believed that he made thunder by riding across the skies in his chariot. Thor was also the protector of all the gods, and what did he use to protect them? A hammer.

Now Thor and his hammer were very close; so close that they never parted. He was so fond of it that he actually gave it a name: Mjolldir.

But one day (and what a day it must have been) he awoke to find his hammer GONE! It had been stolen by the arch enemies of the gods, the *GIANTS!* The only way Thor could get back his hammer was if he could persuade Freyja (the goddess of love) to marry the lord of the giants.

Freyja was desperate for a husband . . . but not *that* desperate. She refused. Now what would Thor do to get his beloved hammer back?

Well, he pretended to be Freyja to fool the giants.

26

He dressed himself up in a wedding gown and wore her distinctive gold necklace. Unfortunately, Thor was very manly ... he had a beard and absolutely huge muscles, but *this* didn't give him away! What did? Well, at the feast he ate rather like a *pig*. Yes, Thor put away ...

- eight whole salmon
- one whole ox
- washed down with three *barrels* of mead!

After this show, Thor's hammer was brought into the feast to bless the bride. Thor could restrain himself no longer, he jumped up to say hello to his best friend. His disguise fell off and he screamed, "I want my hammer back!" After a fight, the big soft lump got his hammer back, never to lose it again.

There are two lessons to be learned from this story. If you meet a Norse god ...

1 Don't ask him to dinner
2 Don't steal his favourite toy

27

VICIOUS VIKING TIMES

Some people get upset if you say the Vikings were vicious. They argue that the Vikings were a cuddly, loveable people who were really quite clever. For example, did you know that Vikings were great inventors? It's true! They liked to invent new ways for people to die! They lived in pretty vicious times. Can you match the following people to their sticky ends?

1 King Edmund didn't want to fight against the Vikings in 869 AD. He wanted to talk to the Viking leader and convert him to Christianity. The Viking leader wanted to stick to the worship of Odin, so King Edmund was . . .

2 An English woman made a wax model of her hated neighbour and stuck an iron pin through its heart. She was accused of being a witch in 900. The accused woman was . . .

3 King Edward was assassinated by the servants of his own mother. She wanted her younger son, Athelred, to become king in 978. King Edward arrived to visit his mother without a bodyguard and he was ... .

4 In 997 King Kenneth of Scotland wanted his son to be king after he died. The other Scottish nobles didn't like this idea. Kenneth was lured to a castle where he was feasted and given lots of wine, then he was . . .

5 In 1012 the Archbishop of Canterbury, Alfheah, was captured by the Danish Viking invaders. They asked for a ransom of silver. Alfheah refused to let his friends pay a ransom, so he was . . .

6 The Irish King, Brian Boru, was killed while he prayed in a wood. The killer, the Viking Brodir, was captured and he was . . .

a) Stabbed. Had one foot twisted in the stirrup of a horse's saddle. The horse was sent charging off, dragging the victim to a bumpy death

b) Taken to a room with a booby-trapped statue. When the statue was touched, several hidden crossbows were set off. The victim died in a hail of bolts

c) Beaten. Tied to a tree and shot full of arrows. Cut down and cut up! Beheaded. Had head and body thrown into a wood

d) Pelted with cattle bones and finished off with a single blow from an axe

e) Drowned in the River Thames at London Bridge
f) Cut open. The victim's intestines were attached to an oak tree and the victim led around the tree as the intestines unwound

Answers:*
1 = c)   2 = e)   3 = a)   4 = b)   5 = d)   6 = f)

* Be careful! The Viking sagas were written a long time after the events happened. They may not be true. And the Vikings may have made up stories about terrible tortures in order to make them sound more brave and fierce than they really were!

The Saxon historians simply said of Edmund's death, "*and they killed the king.*" They don't mention horrible tortures. What do you think?

But one of the unluckiest Vikings was Sigurd the powerful. He was killed by a dead man! Sigurd killed the man in battle, cut off his head and threw it over his saddle as a trophy. But the tooth of the dead man's skull scratched Sigurd's leg. The scratch became infected . . . and Sigurd died!

(Genuine) ancient English joke

When monks weren't writing books they were writing riddles like this one:

> WHAT HAS TWO EARS AND ONE EYE TWO FEET AND 1,200 HEADS, ONE BELLY ONE BACK, ONE PAIR OF HANDS AND ARMS AND ONE NECK?

> A ONE-EYED GARLIC SELLER WITH 1,200 HEADS OF GARLIC TO SELL

(No wonder you don't see many laughing monks with jokes like that! And no wonder the Vikings wanted to exterminate them!)

Vicious Viking medicine

Leif Erikson was probably the first European to land in America – so *there*, Columbus!

LOOK WHAT I GOT FROM THOSE FUNNY INDIANS

The Vikings called it Vinland – maybe because they found wild grapes on "vines" – Vine-land, get it? Or maybe it was because there's a Norse word, "*vin*", meaning "pasture".

Leif left and told his brother, Thorvald, of the discovery. Thorvald and a crew of 35 reached the shores of Vinland (Newfoundland) in the Spring of 1004. After making winter camp they ventured forth, first sailing east then north along the coast.

Thorvald and his crew met native American Indians. The Vikings called them the "Skraelings". During a major battle with the Skraelings, Thorvald was wounded by an arrow in the stomach. What happened next? Did his men:

a) call an ambulance?

b) put him out of his misery

c) try a little bit of Viking first-aid?

Answer: c) This is what Thorvald's men did . . .

CHAPTER 71
~AN ARROW IN THE GUT~

1 Cover victim with a cloak to keep him warm and comfortable

2 Give him this special meal: mix porridge oats with onions and herbs, then feed to the patient, forcibly if necessary

3 Wait until the food is digested

4 Smell the open wound. If it smells of onions and herbs, the intestines have been pierced and the victim will die. If not, patch him up.

5 Contact Odin, the father of all gods, and prepare the Viking for Valhalla (heaven, remember?)

By the way . . . Thorvald died.

Vicious Viking vessels

The Vikings couldn't have carried out those raids on England – and Ireland – if they hadn't been great sailors and built superb boats. They went still further – to Iceland, Greenland and even North America.

The Viking ships are admired for their low, sleek look. But they weren't always like that. The story goes that one man bravely changed the shape of the Viking longboat. This is supposed to be a true story . . .

ONE DAY A KING CAME TO INSPECT HIS NEW SHIP

WHAT A MESS!

THERE WERE DEEP NOTCHES IN THE GUNWALE OF THE SHIP

WHO MADE THESE CHIPS?!!

I D-D-DUNNO YOUR HIGHNESS. I DON'T LIKE CHIPS

WHOEVER DID WILL LOSE HIS HEAD!

EXCUSE ME YOUR HIGHNESS BUT I KNOW WHO DID IT!

YOU DO? GOOD HONEST THORBERG. TELL ME!

ACTUALLY I DID IT!

I'M SHOCKED THORBERG. SHAVE THOSE CHIPS OFF OR I'LL SHAVE YOUR HEAD OFF – AT THE NECK!

SO THORBERG PARED THE SIDES UNTIL THE NOTCHES DISAPPEARED. THE SIDES NOW DIPPED LOWER

WHAT AN IMPROVEMENT

REMEMBER FOLKS... CHIPS MAKE DIPS IN SHIPS FOR FASTER TRIPS!

Build a Longboat – Ten Top Tips

1 Choose a spot near the sea.[1]

2 Choose your trees . . . watch the way they grow so you pick the ones that give the shapes you need.[2]

3 Pick straight oak trees for the keel – the backbone of the ship.[3]

4 Build "ribs" at right angles to this backbone.[4]

5 Cut down a few dozen pine trees for the planks – split the trunks into planks by hammering in wedges.[5]

6 Drill holes in the planks to take the nails.[6]

7 Nail the planks to the ribs.[7]

8 Overlap the planks until you have built the complete boat.[8]

1 Well, you wouldn't want to carry the boat fifty miles to the sea when it's finished, would you?

2 Trees can take hundreds of years to grow. It's better if you don't spend hundreds of years watching them.

3 Oaks are getting rare. Cut one down in modern Britain and you may end up in jail.

4 They're called *ribs* because they look like, well, ribs – the boat now looks like the skeleton of a dinosaur, lying on its back.

5 No, you can't use electric saws because they haven't been invented.

6 And no electric drills either, you wimp!

7 If you ask a teacher to hold the nails then you won't hit your thumb.

8 But don't launch it yet! It will sink!

9 Find a cow (or a sheep), and make ropes from the hair, dip the ropes in tar and pack the joins with the tarry rope and leave them to dry.[1]

10 Carve a **really** ugly face on the front.[2]

You're ready to fit the oars, the mast, the steering oar, and the sail.

Get a crew of muscular sailors and invade somebody!

OVERLAPPING PINE PLANKS

TARRING JOINS

PLANKS A LOT

UGLY FIGUREHEAD

SPLITTING LOGS FOR PLANKS

Did you know . . . ?

Ships carried tents and frames. The ends of each tent were carved with faces of fierce animals. These scared evil spirits away. The sailors could pitch the tents on the ship when they stopped for the night. But usually the sailors went ashore and snuggled into their leather sleeping bags . . . and sometimes they shared a sleeping bag to keep warm!

1   This is messy. Do NOT wear your best clothes.
2   A picture of your teacher will give you something to copy from.

THE POWER OF VIKING POEMS

The first people to inhabit the British Isles were the battling Britons. Then along came the rotten Romans who drove the native British into the wet and western wildernesses of Wales. But the Romans went home in the fifth century AD to help defend the Roman Empire nearer home.

So the Angles, Saxons and Jutes moved in from northern Europe. You might have thought they'd be *glad* to find a deserted country to move into. But they were actually rather sad when they saw the ruined Roman towns. One of them wrote a poem called . . .

The ruin
How fearsome is this old wall,
Crushed and torn by time.
And great town buildings broken,
Work of giants dying.

Tumbling towers and fine roofs,
Broken down old gates.
Ceilings fallen, torn apart
By the hand of Fate.

Great bright inn and bath house,
Banquets in the hall
Once were filled with laughter.
Time put paid to all.

But 300 years later it was the Anglo-Saxons' turn to have their homes wrecked. By the Vikings. And those Vikings thought that poetry was pretty important too. One Viking even thought it could save his life. But did it . . . ?

The best poem of Egil's life

Eric Bloodaxe was well named. He was king because he'd killed off all his rivals – including a few half-brothers. But he still had one deadly rival . . . Egil Skallagrimsson!

Then, in 949 AD, Eric Bloodaxe had the most pleasant shock of his murderous life. The doors of the royal hall in York opened and a breathless servant scuttled in.

"King Eric, your highness, you have a visitor, sire."

Queen Gunnhild looked icicles at the humble man and her voice grated, "Who is it? Speak up!"

"Er . . . he says he's Egil Skallagrimsson, your highness!"

The pale queen turned whiter than a rat's tooth. "Impossible. He wouldn't dare come here . . . not unless he has an army with him!"

"No, your highness – just a couple of servants!" the miserable man mumbled.

"Then have him killed!" the queen hissed.

"Yes, your highness," the man said with a bow that brushed the floor.

"No, don't!" King Eric ordered.

"No, your highness," the simpering servant snivelled.

The queen glared at her husband. "You've waited ten years for this chance!" she cried.

Eric nodded. "So another hour won't make any difference. I want to see this man."

Gunnhild rose to her feet. A spot of colour glowed in her frozen face. "Have you forgotten what Egil Skallagrimsson has done? Killed your friends and family – yes, killed your own son. He has scorned you and insulted your royal person. He has to die."

"Later," the king said calmly. "First let's hear what he has to say." He looked at a guard. "Have Egil Skallagrimsson brought before me," he ordered.

Egil was unarmed and half-smiling as he was led before the royal couple.

"I thought you were hiding in Iceland," Queen Gunnhild sneered. "What are you doing in England?"

"I came to see my friend Athelstan of the English," Egil answered quietly.

"Athelstan? Athelstan's been dead for ten years," Gunnhild gasped.

The prisoner shrugged. "So I've heard. But news travels slowly in Iceland."

"So you decided to pay us a visit instead," Eric Bloodaxe said.

"No. I decided to go back home. But a storm wrecked me on the coast not far from here," Egil explained.

"The gods will it. It is a punishment for your evil deeds," the queen said smugly.

"Perhaps," the prisoner agreed. "But I escaped the wreck. Perhaps the gods wanted me to live!"

"Or perhaps drowning is too quick for you," Gunnhild grated. "Perhaps they want you to have a nice slow death at the hands of Eric!"

"Eric is a Viking. He knows that fame is not bought cheaply. He would gain no fame from killing me now. If I'd tried to run from the shipwreck and hide like a common criminal, then Eric could have had me killed. But I came here freely, knowing Eric will treat me fairly. Then he will win word-fame."

Gunnhild began to speak but her husband silenced her with a wave of his hand. "Tonight I feast. Tomorrow I decide what to do with you. You may spend the night as my guest . . . in a cellar teeming with toads. Guards! Take him away."

And while Eric Bloodaxe feasted and slept, his enemy worked on his greatest art. His poetry.

HEY! THAT'S NOT HALF BAD

The next morning the proud prisoner stood before the royal couple. "Your highness," he said boldly. "Before you decide my fate, I ask you one favour."

"Kill him," Gunnhild groaned.

"No. Go on, Egil Skallagrimsson," Eric insisted.

"Allow me to recite a poem I have written to celebrate your fame. The people in this hall can hear it. My poem will bring you more than my death ever could. It will bring you word-fame."

"Kill him," Gunnhild shrilled.

"We will hear this poem," Eric said. "We can always kill him later."

And the court of King Eric gathered round the Icelander and listened. He chanted 20 verses he'd written in his head the night before. He began . . .

Listen, O king, what honour I bring;
Silence I ask while I play out my task.
Your brave deeds I'll tell, which all men know well.
Only Odin can say where the men you killed lay.

He went on to describe Eric's valour in battle . . .
Then Egil changed the rhyme pattern and made his
listeners wonder at his skill.

> *I praise this king in his own land,*
> *I gladly sing of his just hand.*
> *A hand so free with golden gains,*
> *But strongly he can rule his Danes.*

He finished . . .

> *To praise this lord, my dumb lips broke;*
> *The words out-poured, my still tongue spoke.*
> *From my poet's breast these words took wing,*
> *Now all the rest may his praise sing.*

There was a silence in the great royal hall when Egil
had finished. At last it was broken by one harsh
voice. "Kill him," Gunnhild said.

The Viking listeners muttered angrily. One spoke
boldly, "King Eric, this man's poem will bring you
word-fame. Your name will live forever. In return
you should grant him his life."

"Kill him," Gunnhild said.

"I will decide," Eric Bloodaxe said.

But what did Eric decide? Was the Viking love of
word-fame so important? Or was his wife right – the
Viking love of vengeance should come first?

Answer: In return for the poem, Eric gave Egil
his life.

40

Egil's poem was typical of many. The Viking poems gloried in death and destruction. One poet wrote this to the gory glory of war . . .

> *I have held a sword and spear*
> *When they were slippery with blood.*
> *Hawks were hovering at the kill,*
> *As brave the violent Vikings stood.*
>
> *Red flames swallowed up men's roofs*
> *As we raged and cut them down;*
> *Bodies, skewered, lay there sleepy*
> *In the gateways of the town.*

But the Vikings didn't always win . . .

VICIOUS VIKINGS
VANQUISHED

Someone with a few brains could beat the Vikings. Here are some battles the Vikings would rather forget . . .

1 The Battle of Ashdown

The Wessex Star

A RIGHT RIVETING READ
April 871

YOUNG ROYAL LEADS ROUT AT READING

The Wessex Saxons washed their swords in Viking blood last night to celebrate a vital victory. And the surprise star of the battle was ex-king Athelwulf's youngest son, Alfred. Young Alfred showed big brother Athelred how to give the Danes a drubbing. The young Wessex Wonder was meant to lead half of the Saxon swordsmen, while Athelred was to lead the rest.

Imagine the popular prince's surprise when he went to King Athelred's tent and found his brother praying.

"There's a battle to be fought out there, brother!" Alf argued.

"I serve God first and men second," the crazy king replied.

So brave Alf decided to go it alone.

The Danes were favourites in the fight. They held the high ground. But Awesome Alf went at them "like a wild boar", one witness raved.

The bloody battle raged around a single stunted thorn bush. Saxons and Danes swapped places as both tried to hit that hilly height. At last the sword-swinging Saxons drove the desperate Danes back to their camp till darkness stopped the slaughter.

The Wessex Star says, "Move over, Athelred. Let's make Kid Alfred King Alfred!"

The Wessex Star's own poet wrote this ode to the great victory . . .

Ode to Alf who cuts Vikings in half

Our Alfie's the hero of
   Reading,
For he jumped like a
   flea from his bedding,
While King Athelred
   prayed
Good prince Alfred
   just slayed
Till the Danes were
   left bledding and
   dedding!

Note: Poor Athelred died soon after the Battle of Ashdown and young Alfred became King.

43

2 The Battle of Stamford Bridge

THE SAXON SUN

STILL ONLY 20 PENNIES

25 SEP 1066

A GOOD WIN, SON!

Heroic Harold Godwinsson has defeated the nasty Norwegians in the North of England. Yesterday, the Horrible Hardrada was stuffed at Stamford Bridge. Saxon England is free of those vile Vikings at last.

Godwinsson (known to his men as Gozza) admitted last night, "We had a bit of luck – but then, you need a bit of luck to beat the likes of Hardrada. The lads call him, Hard-as-nails Hardrada."

The "bit of luck" the great Godwinsson referred to was an incredible mistake made by hopeless Hardrada. The Norwegian ninny thought the Saxons were down in London, so he gave his men a bit of a holiday. One of the few Viking survivors described the scene to our reporter. "We was sunbathing, like. No armour – no nothing! Then we saw a cloud of dust and the sunshine on the spears. Well, we thought it was a bunch of our mates coming up from the ships, didn't we? I'd just turned over to tan the other side when they jumped on us! I couldn't find me trousers, never mind me sword. Sick as a parrot I was!"

The super Saxons tried to cross the river to get at Hardrada himself. A nutty Norwegian (a Berserker with a battle-axe) was on the bridge and battered a few of our brave lads. He also gave Hardrada time to warn his other warriors.

"Gave us a hard time," a Saxon survivor said. "Bit of a blood-bath, really. Hardrada asked Godwinsson for land but the boss just replied he'd give the Norwegian seven foot – enough for a grave . . . get it? Laugh? The lads nearly died . . . well, a lot of them did die, of course. But we won in the end."

Hardrada died in the fight. Now gutsy Godwinsson faces a new fight at the other end of the country. Our continental correspondent says that William of Normandy is planning an invasion on the south coast.

But *The Saxon Sun* says Harold will nobble the Normans in no time! That'll be one in the eye for William!

Editorial

The Saxon Sun Editor says . . .

Three cheers for brave Harold. He deserves an ode – so here's one what I wrote. We believe the people of England should sing this patriotic piece as he heads south to face William the Norman . . .

God save our gracious
      King
He done some real good
      things,
God save the King.
Send him a load of cash
As to the south he'll dash
To give old Willi-um a
      bash!
God save the King!

The Saxon Sun is offering two free tickets to the battle against the Normans, yes TWO, to the reader who comes up with the best tune for this stirring battle song.

45

LIVE LIKE A VIKING

To understand history we have to try to understand the people who lived it. Can you get inside the mind of a Viking? Can you make the same decisions a Viking would have made . . .?

Think like a Viking 1: AD 980 – - Eiric's Story

Nothing is so sad as a beaten Viking. Nothing so mad. Nothing so dangerous!

Eiric was sad. To be beaten by the Norwegians in the battle of Hjorungavagr was bad enough. To be one of the 70 survivors was shameful. Eiric would rather have died in the battle. Instead he was a prisoner. Taken alive and tied with ropes to his comrades. The young man was mad . . .

"Why can't they give us a weapon and let us die fighting?" young Eiric cried.

The old warrior, Bjorn, next to him, looked at the boy wearily. "How old are you, Eiric?"

"Eighteen," Eiric answered.

"How did you live so long and be so stupid?"

Eiric's pale face turned red. "Why do you say that?"

"Because it is obvious, boy. They don't want us to die bravely. They want us to die as cowards. They want us to die pleading for our lives. They want to show that the Vikings are weak. It makes the Norwegians look strong."

Eiric nodded. "But we will not die weakly. We will die as heroes."

"Better not to die at all," Bjorn sighed. "I've a wife and children who'll suffer when I'm dead. You've a mother and a father, haven't you?"

The young man turned his ice-blue eyes to the winter sky. "Yes," he said shortly.

"I don't fear death any more than the next Viking – but still it makes me sad to think of the ones we leave behind. Be brave . . . but be sad, young Eiric."

Eiric stared at the frozen ground and went silent while a flock of gulls screeched and circled overhead, sensing that death was in the Yuletide air. The young warrior struggled with the thick rope that bound him to Bjorn.

The old man shook his head. He chanted an old poem softly . . .

It is frightful now
To look around
As a blood-red cloud
Shadows the sky

The ropes were too strong. Eiric shook back his long, fair hair and said, "There is no shame in cheating death, then?"

"And how would you do that?" Bjorn asked tiredly.

Before his young friend could answer, the rope was tugged sharply and the line of captured Vikings was dragged to its feet.

Earl Hakon of Norway marched cheerfully down the line and called, "Does any man wish me to spare his life? All he has to do is ask, politely, and swear to become a slave to Norway!"

The Viking warriors stared at him with contempt. "Prepare to die," he sneered and nodded to a Norwegian soldier.

The first Viking was freed from the rope. He stepped forward, thrust his chin out and waited for the sweep of the sword. As his head was severed the Viking warriors cheered.

"Well died!" a huge warrior laughed and stepped forward to be executed. His hair was grey as the December sky. He turned to his comrades. "My friends!" he cried. "There is a better life after death!" He pulled a dagger from his belt. "When my head is off I will raise this dagger in the air."

He stretched out his arms and waited. As the sword fell . . . so did the knife in the huge Viking's hand. The cheer this time was softer. Bjorn sighed.

Another brave man stepped forward. He too turned to the waiting men and spoke. "We will show them how a Viking dies! Executioner . . . strike me in the face. You will see that I do not turn pale!"

The sword fell. His face did not turn pale . . . but the Vikings saw that the man closed his eyes at the moment of death. The cheer this time was soft as the whisper of steel on ice.

Eiric jumped to his feet. He had to gamble on his plan to save the lives of the other 67 men. "Me next!"

When the Vikings saw their youngest step forward they struggled with the ropes and argued, "No! Me! No! Me!"

Sneering Hakon cried, "Kill the boy!"

"Wait!" Eiric said. "I do not want my hair to blunt your sword. Have one of your men hold my hair up while the sword falls on my neck."

The Norwegian Earl grinned and ordered a soldier to twist Eiric's long hair round his hands.

The Vikings fell silent. The swordsman raised his sword. The sword swept through the air like a longboat through the water.

At the last instant Eiric jerked back his head sharply. He dragged down the arms of the soldier who held his hair. Dragged them down into the path of the sword.

The soldier screamed as the steel bit into his wrists.

The Vikings roared.

Earl Hakon laughed. "Young man, for that entertainment you deserve to live. Set him free!"

Eiric's life was saved.

And so the story might have ended . . . but this is a *Viking* story.

If you were a Viking, how would you want it to end?

a) Eiric goes home to his farm and lives a long and peaceful life.
b) Eiric refuses to accept the pardon unless the other Vikings are allowed to go free. Earl Hakon admires his bravery and all the remaining Vikings are spared.
c) Eiric refuses to accept the pardon unless the other Vikings are allowed to go free. Earl Hakon refuses and the boy is executed along with all the others.

Think like a Viking 2

An old Viking poem gives advice on how to behave if you want to be a good Viking.

> *Do not laugh at the old and grey*
> *There may be wise things they have to say!*

(This doesn't apply to *teachers*. Vikings didn't have teachers so they wouldn't know.)

> *When a guest comes to your home*
> *Give them a wash and a seat nice and warm.*

(And never insist on showing them your holiday video or you'll bore the socks off them.)

> *Beer and mead are not that good,*
> *They make your brain as thick as mud.*

(And some people are as thick as mud even without beer and mead.)

> *A coward hides – at home he'll stay*
> *But time will kill him anyway!*

(But he'll still last longer than a warrior who goes out looking for a punch-up.)

> *A man who wants to kill his foe*
> *Must get up quick and never slow.*
> *A wolf that wants to have a snack*
> *Does not lie sleeping on his back.*

(Or ... "Late to rise, late to bed, could make you healthy, wealthy and dead!" And this is why teachers get to school before their pupils.)

> *Cows and friends and parents die*
> *After some years so will I.*
> *One thing that will live the same*
> *Is a hero's famous name.*

(Not to mention the time you made a fool of yourself by being sick at your cousin's birthday party. Why do people never let you forget that?)

> *You never can tell who is out to get you;*
> *So look round a doorway before you step through.*

(And look *above* the door in case somebody's balanced a bucket of water over the top.)

> *When you go in the fields take your sword*
>   *and your spear;*
> *For some day an enemy just might appear.*

(This does not mean you have to take a weapon with you when you play football or hockey!)

51

Think like a Viking 3

That same Viking poem gave another piece of advice. It said . . .

Even a handless man can herd sheep,
But a corpse is no good to anyone.

So, when they faced a fight they were sure to lose, they didn't waste their lives attacking. Instead they used trickery.

Hastein and his Vikings were probably the first to sail into the Mediterranean Sea. At last they found a great fortress of gleaming white marble . . .

ROME! THE GREATEST CITY IN THE WORLD! BUT WE'LL NEVER TAKE IT ALIVE!

AND AS WE VIKINGS ALWAYS SAY, A CORPSE IS NO GOOD TO ANYBODY!

GREAT IDEA, UBBI... GET ME A COFFIN I HAVE A PLAN!

A PLAN?

SO UBBI WENT TO THE GATES OF THE CITY AND ASKED TO SEE THE BISHOP.

MY LEADER, HASTEIN, IS OLD AND SICK

53

The Luna massacre was a story told by an Italian historian, not a Viking. But modern historians think it's unlikely to have happened that way. By the time Hastein reached Luna in the ninth century, that city was in ruins anyway. And no Viking remains have ever been found there. Hastein *did* attack towns in the Mediterranean – but he never reached Rome.

Eric the Red – *This is Your Life*

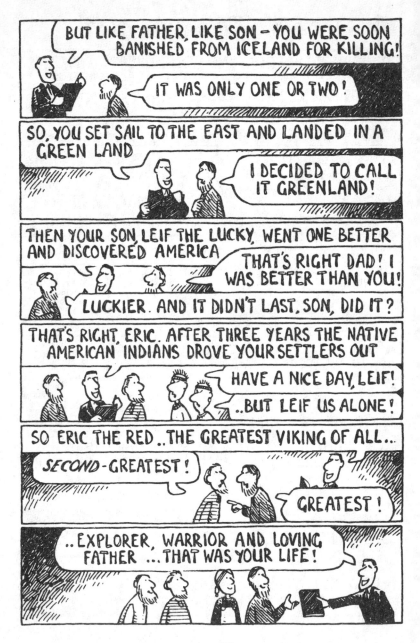

Would *you* make a good Viking?

Answer the following questions to see how good a Viking you would be . . .

1 You come home for a meal. What would you prefer?

a) A bag of crisps

b) Bread and cheese

c) Raw polar bear meat

2 Somebody calls your sister "Reindeer-face". What do you do?

a) Agree

b) Hit them

c) Kill them

3 Your wife wears your trousers. What do you do?

a) Wear her dress to get your own back

b) Take them back

c) Divorce her

4 How would you like your bath?

a) Hot with foam

b) In cold water

c) In a steam bath until the dirt runs off with the sweat followed by a roll in deep snow.

5 What is your favourite entertainment?

a) Reading a book

b) Listening to a good story – an exciting one with lots of fighting and dying

c) Picking a fight with someone and wrestling until you're exhausted.

6 You go to a wedding. How long does it take you to enjoy your meal?

a) An hour

b) A day

c) A month

7 You go to a feast and drink strong ale and mead. When do you stop?
a) When you've had enough
b) When you're drunk
c) When you're totally unconscious
8 What is the most entertaining use for horses?
a) Pony trekking
b) Racing
c) Training them to fight one another to the death
9 What would you wear as you went into battle?
a) A bullet-proof vest under a suit of armour
b) A coat of chain mail and a helmet
c) Nothing except a small piece of animal skin to give you the strength of that animal
10 What would you use instead of toilet paper?
a) Yesterday's newspaper
b) Moss
c) Don't use anything

WHAT! NO MOSS!

HERE BUNNY BUNNY BUNNY

Answers:
Any a) answers: Sorry, forget it! You'll never make a Viking. Just be glad you were born in the twentieth century.
Any b) answers: Yes. The Vikings would do all these things. You will make a Viking . . . but not a very good one.
Any c) answers: You're as vicious as a Viking as Erik the Red!
More than seven answers (c) . . . I'm only glad I'm not your teacher!

Viking names

Would you rather be an Orm, an Ulf or a Bjorn? Or maybe even an Ulfbjorn? If so, you'd be named after an animal.

Orm is a snake

Ulf is a wolf

Bjorn is a bear

So you can work out for yourself what an *Ulfbjorn* was!

Vikings were named after gods – Thor was very popular. Many Viking names are still in use in Britain today – Rolf, Harold and Eric for example. But the great Vikings are known in history by their nicknames. For example, one king is known to us as Harold Fine-hair . . .

Harry's Horrible Hair

The story goes that young Prince Harold fancied a beautiful princess called Gytha.

"Marry me," he begged.

But beautiful Gytha didn't fancy a poor young prince. "Ask me again when you have a proper kingdom to call your own."

Harold swore that he wouldn't cut or comb his hair until he'd made himself ruler of all of Norway. It took him ten years, but he succeeded. Imagine the state of his hair by then! But he won Gytha, so it was all worthwhile.

Then Harold went to the baths and had his hair trimmed, washed and combed. Everyone agreed that he had a fine head of hair. His name changed to Harold Fine-hair. Before, it was Harold Mop-hair!

What name would you give yourself or your friends ... or your teachers? Test your teacher. Which of the following were *really* the names of Vikings?

True or false?

1. HARALD REDBEARD
2. OLAF THE STOUT
3. KON SMELLY-FEET
4. IVAR THE BONELESS
5. SVEIN FORKBEARD
6. ODIN PUDDING-FACE
7. HAROLD BLUETOOTH
8. KEITH FLATNOSE
9. OLAF THE PEACOCK
10. RAGNAR HAIRY BREECHES
11. SIGURD SNAKE-IN-THE-EYE
12. RUDOLPH THE RED-NOSE
13. SIGTRYGG SILK-BEARD
14. SIGRID THE AMBITIOUS
15. FLOKI RAVENS
16. ASGOT THE CLUMSY
17. GLUM
18. CONAN THE LIBRARIAN
19. SIGTRYGG ONE-EYE
20. THOROLF BUTTER

Answer: All are true except 3, 6, 12 and 18

60

Several of these names belonged to very famous Vikings – Olaf the Stout and Ivar the Boneless, for example. Your teacher probably knows those. But, what teacher *doesn't* tell you . . . because they don't *know* . . . is that the Vikings *weren't* usually known by these nicknames when they were alive! The nicknames were usually invented by history writers in the Middle Ages to describe the different Vikings. So, it would *not* have been a good idea to go up to Viking Keith and say, "Good morning, Mr Flatnose!" The reply might have had something to do with the flattening of your own nose!

THERE GOES KEITH – REALLY-QUITE-A-NICE-NOSE-WHEN-YOU-LOOK-CLOSELY

Write like a Viking

1   Viking letters were known as Runes. Vikings scratched their runes on wood or stone. It's easier to scratch straight lines than curves. So runes were made up of straight lines.

2   The runes would be used by fortune-tellers who moved from village to village giving people horoscopes.

3   Fortune-tellers were so popular they always got the best food and drink!

4   Fortune-tellers like Kon deserved it. According to a sage . . .

> *The youthful Kon knew all the runes*
> *Runes everlasting, runes life-giving;*
> *Knew also how to save men's lives,*
> *Blunt the sword blades, calm the wild waves,*
> *Could understand the cries of birds;*
> *Could put out flames and quieten sorrows.*

5   Some historians say the rune alphabet was also used for magic. Charms, spells and curses would be written in runes. But the truth is they are only guessing this because some runes couldn't be understood! Most messages were simply everyday business, rather the way someone at home might leave you a message, such as "Don't forget to feed the stick insects" or "Your dinner's in the cat".

6 The rune alphabet was known as the *futhark*. But the order of the letters was quite different to our own alphabet, which is based on the Latin. We learn a-b-c-d-e, the Vikings learned f-u-th-a-r-k.

7 The Viking stories, sagas, weren't written in runes – they were memorised and recited by poets. They were finally written down 200 years after the Viking attacks had finished. They were written in Latin.

8 Twentieth century writers such as J R R Tolkien have used the idea of runes as a secret language. In his book, *The Hobbit*, the runes are the writing of the dwarves.

9 Some runic inscriptions can still be found on stones by the roadside in Scandinavia. They were written on all sorts of things found in the Viking household, because quill pens, ink and parchment (used by the monks in those days) were too expensive. The sort of things that have been found include:

"*Kiss me*" on a piece of bone.

"*Odin*" on a piece of human skull! A sacrifice perhaps?

The word "*kabr*" on a comb . . . and *kabr* means comb!

I CAUGHT HIM TRYING TO CARVE "CAT" ON THE CAT

10 Around the year 800 AD the runic alphabet was reduced to just 16 letters. This is very confusing for us because one letter can have several sounds – you just have to work out which! For example "u" rune can be read as u, oo, y, w, or o. No one knows why the alphabet was shortened in this way.

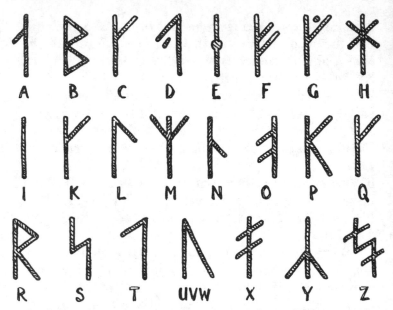

And here's a rune message . . . or it could be a rude message! What would this mean if it was written by a Saxon on a Viking wall . . . ?

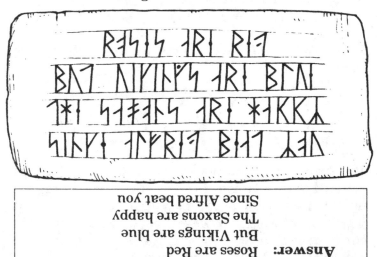

Wash like a Viking

If you decided to wash – and most Vikings did, once a week on a Saturday night – then you'd need some soap. You couldn't pop down to Boots the Chemist to buy some, though. You had to make it yourself. If you want to know what it was like then try this recipe . . .

Make your own Viking soap

1   Peel and mash up some conkers.

2   Add some water.

3   Squeeze out extra water.

4   Mould into the shape of soap.

5   Leave to dry.

6   Use as soap.

Look like a Viking

Maybe you'd like to look like a Viking. Perhaps you're off to a fancy dress party . . . perhaps you want to make a play about Vikings . . . or perhaps you just want to attack a monastery. (Take a bag of chips and then you can say, "Have a chip, monk!") Starting from the floor you'd dress like this . . .

Shoes: Vikings wore shoes of soft leather. But sometimes they left the fur of the animals on! Cover your own shoes with some furry material to give the same effect.

Trousers: can be narrow or baggy – the Vikings wore all sorts. Wear an old pair then wind strips of cloth up to the knee in a criss-cross pattern.

Kirtles (knee-length shirts): borrow a large, old shirt. Remove the collar or turn it inside the neck. Leave it hanging outside the trousers. Put a plain leather belt around the waist. (The Viking shirts were made of wool and could be dyed a single colour. They could be embroidered with silk or metal threads.)

Cloak: use a woollen blanket. Fasten at the neck with a brooch. (The Vikings used rough woollen cloaks and they also used animal skins. Wearing animal skins is considered cruel these days . . . so keep your hands off the neighbour's hamster – it would be too small anyway!)

Head gear: the Vikings wore long hair and long moustaches or neatly trimmed beards. (No. Not the women, stupid!) On their heads they wore hoods or fur caps. Of course, when they went into battle, they wore helmets.

66

VIKING WOMEN

Would you like to have lived in Viking times? And, if you did, would you like to have been a woman?

Did you know?

Viking women . . .

1   managed the farms while their husbands were away – the chief would hand over his keys before he left.

2   could marry at 12 – but 15 was more usual. Something very odd for those days was that a Viking woman could divorce her husband when she wanted to.
One Viking woman divorced her husband because he showed too much bare chest.

3   would receive a bride-price (cash) from her husband which she kept. She also brought a cash present from her father – but got it back if they divorced.

4   kept their own surnames after marriage.

5   taught daughters to cook, milk cows, churn butter, make cheese, bake bread, brew beer, spin, weave, sew and skin animals – they also learned how to swim and use weapons in case they were attacked. Irish historians told stories of fighting female warriors, but they were probably untrue.

6 could claim land. If a man came to a new country then he could have as much land as he could walk around in one day carrying a flaming torch with him. But, if a woman wanted land then she could have as much as she could walk around in a day leading a two-year-old cow.

7 had names such as . . .

| Sigrid | Thora | Ingrid | Gudrun |
| Tove | Ase | Ragnhild | Gunnhild |

8 were banned from longboat raids, but when the Vikings planned to settle a land they would take the women with them on the ships. Women didn't become merchants or craft-workers, but it wasn't all bad: there is a record of a Viking woman who won

fame as travelling poet and another as a rune-carver. There is a story of the Red Maiden who was supposed to have been a warrior-princess in north-eastern Ireland for a while, but it's unlikely to be true.

9 were not treated as equal to men in death. While rich men were buried in their longboats, Viking women were often buried in a wagon instead of a coffin!

10 had work which included combing her husband's hair . . . to get rid of the nits!

The bad news for Viking women . . .

. . . the Viking tribes who settled in Russia adopted some of the strange and vicious funeral customs of the native people. The Arab traveller, Ibn Fadlan, described the funeral of a rich member of the Rus tribe.

Ibn Fadlan called this a "Viking" funeral. A lot of historians have said "this is how the Vikings treated their women". That's not true. All this bit of horrible history writing shows is how "Russian Vikings" treated *some* women. Ibn Fadlan wrote . . .

I'd heard a lot about the burial of the Rus Tribe chiefs and wanted to see one for myself. They burned the body in a ship, but that was nothing compared to what else went on! At last I was told of the death of an important man. Now was my chance to see for myself.

The man had several slave girls as wives. When he died his family asked the wives, "Who wants to go with him?"

One woman answered, "I do!"

When the day of the cremation arrived I went down to the river where his ship lay. I noticed they'd pulled it up on to the shore. Then they brought a bed and put it in the ship. They put a mattress on the bed covered with best Greek cloth.

Then along came an old woman who they called The Angel of Death! She's in charge of arranging everything and of killing the slave girl. She was a grim woman, stout and strong.

On the Friday afternoon they placed the dead man on the bed and covered it with a tent. Then they led the slave girl to a frame . . . a bit like a door frame. She placed her feet on the hands of two men who

*lifted her up so she could see over the top of the frame.
"What can you see?" they asked.*

*"I can see my master, sitting in Paradise. He is
calling for me . . . let me go to him!"*

*So they took her to the ship. She slipped off the two
bracelets she was wearing and gave them to the
Angel of Death.*

*The Angel of Death led the girl into the tent. The
men began to beat their shields with sticks so her
cries would not be heard and upset the other women.*

*Then as the men strangled her the Angel of Death
plunged a knife into her heart.*

*The dead man's closest relative took a piece of
lighted wood and set fire to a pile of wood beneath the
ship. Flames swallowed everything – ship, tent, man
and slave-girl.*

*A man turned to me and said, "You Arabs are
stupid!"*

"Why's that?" I asked.

*"Because you bury your loved ones in the ground
where the worms and insects eat them. But we burn
them in an instant so they go straight to Paradise."*

The idea of burning a body seemed to shock Ibn
Fadlan more than the useless death of the slave-girl.

He also described a Rus custom of putting a
favourite wife in a grave with a dead husband. The
entrance to the grave is then blocked and the wife
dies with him.

Today we are used to cremation but would be
horrified at the idea of a woman giving up her life
just because her husband died. BUT . . . this custom
wasn't recorded anywhere else in Viking writings, so
perhaps it was more of a rotten Russian habit than a
vicious Viking one!

70

Trouble with the family

If you had a family then you fought to support it in Viking times. You also fought for friends, leaders and your in-laws. Everyone had so many friends and family that sooner or later they'd be involved in a "Blood Feud" – revenge taken by the shedding of blood.

The trouble was that taking revenge wasn't the end of it. The avenger would then have to be punished by his victim's family who would then be avenged by the avenger's family and . . . well, you get the idea!

Long-running feuds could only end when a referee was called in to judge what was to be done. Everyone agreed his decision would be accepted. He would then decide who had suffered the most and order the other family to pay blood-money. The payment of blood-money would even things up. There were no winners and no losers – honour was even and the feud could end.

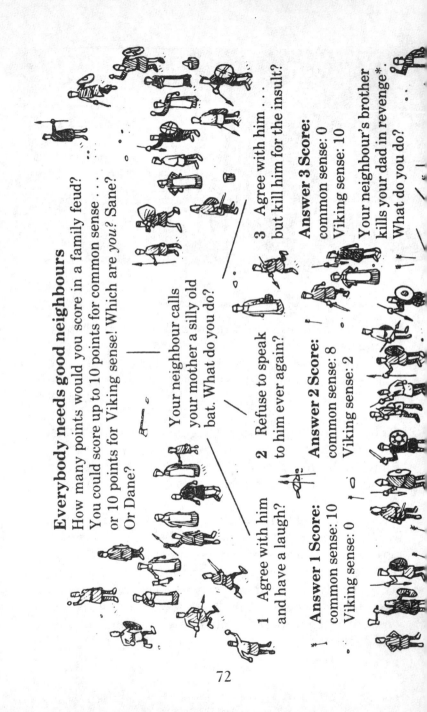

Everybody needs good neighbours

How many points would you score in a family feud? You could score up to 10 points for common sense . . . or 10 points for Viking sense! Which are *you*? Sane? Or Dane?

Your neighbour calls your mother a silly old bat. What do you do?

1 Agree with him and have a laugh?

2 Refuse to speak to him ever again?

3 Agree with him . . . but kill him for the insult?

Answer 1 Score:
common sense: 10
Viking sense: 0

Answer 2 Score:
common sense: 8
Viking sense: 2

Answer 3 Score:
common sense: 0
Viking sense: 10

Your neighbour's brother kills your dad in revenge*. What do you do? . . .

72

a) Demand "Blood Money" – cash for the life of your father?

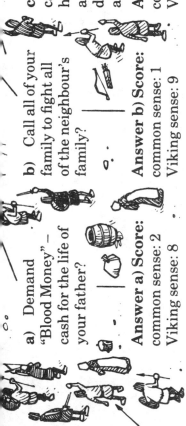

Answer a) Score:
common sense: 2
Viking sense: 8

*When it came to revenge the avengers didn't always pick the killer – they often picked the most important member of the family . . . even if he had nothing whatever to do with the original crime or insult!!

b) Call all of your family to fight all of the neighbour's family?

Answer b) Score:
common sense: 1
Viking sense: 9

c) Have a "Burn-in" – catch the neighbours at home, set fire to their house and give them a choice – die in the fire or come out and die by your swords?**

Answer c) Score:
common sense: 0
Viking sense: 10

**If you married into a feuding family you could choose whether or not you wanted to be part of the feud. A Viking woman who chose to die with her husband was Bergthora. Enemies set fire to her home in order to kill Njal, her husband, and her sons. They called to Bergthora to come outside and she would be spared. She came out and said, "When I married Njal I promised that we would share the same fate." Then she walked back inside to die with him.

73

Not all Viking women felt the same loyalty as Bergthora. Especially when their husbands had been bullies! Njal's best friend was Gunnar. And his wife had *quite* a different way of behaving when enemies came knocking on the door . . .

Hallgerd's diary

My husband Gunnar was Trouble. That's right . . . with a capital "T". Whenever there was a fight in Bergthorshvoll then you could be sure Gunnar was in the middle of it. He was a bully and a trouble-maker. Once – just once – he slapped me on the face. I couldn't hit him back. But I could wait for my revenge, couldn't I?

The day came when the council sentenced Gunnar to be exiled for three years. That meant he could leave Iceland, and live, or he could stay and the law would not stop his enemies from killing him. And believe me, Gunnar had enemies!

He decided to leave, but a strange thing happened. As he rode to the quay where his boat was moored, his horse stumbled. He fell over its head and landed on his feet . . . facing the way he had come. He took

LOOK DADDY! AN ACROBAT

one look back at his beloved farm and said, "Right! That's it! I'm not going." And he came back home.

Word got around and by nightfall the house was surrounded. Now, not even Gunnar could fight 100 men with his sword. But he *could* stay in the house and defend himself with his bow and arrows.

That's what he did. Until suddenly his bowstring snapped. "That's done it," he sighed. "I'm a dead man."

"Shame," I said.

Then he looked at me sort of funny. He reached out a hand and stroked my hair. "Lovely hair," he muttered.

"Thanks very much," I said. "It's not like you to pay me a compliment."

"I was just thinking. That hair would make me a wonderful new bowstring!"

"Would it?" I smiled.

"It would." He raised his knife. "Can I take a piece?"

"Remember the day you slapped my face?" I asked.

"What sort of answer is that?" he asked.

"It's the sort of answer that means 'NO'!" I told him.

"You shall not be asked again," he said. And he went out to die like a Viking. I'll say that for him. He died well.

But I'll say something else — and you men take note — he'll not be slapping me on the face again!

VIKING CHILDREN

You may complain about Terrible Teachers and Pain-in-the-neck Parents. But life as a Viking child would have been harder than yours. For a start, childhood would have been short. The boys would begin raiding as soon as they were old enough and the girls would be farming and doing housework for most of their lives. Life was particularly horrible for the Viking slave classes – the thralls.

Children's lesson no. 1: Don't get yourself born as a thrall!

A Viking writer described thralls as . . .

> *Wrinkled hands and knobbled knuckles,*
> *Fingers thick and face foul-looking,*
> *Back bowed down, and big flat feet.*

(Does that sound like anyone you know?)

Graveyard queue
A thrall's life was not a happy one.
She/he had to work on the land to make a living, but she/he also had to work for a master for no pay! And what work!

A male slave would . . .
- build walls
- cover the fields with manure
- herd pigs and goats
- dig peat (a sort of turf burned for fuel)

A female slave would . . .
- grind corn by hand
- milk cows and goats
- make cheese
- cook
- wash

Thralls had to have their master's permission to get married. They couldn't go anywhere without permission. But a thrall could work hard and buy his freedom. Apart from freedom in life he even got a better *death!* The Christian laws of south-east Norway give an order for burying people in the graveyard . . .

- the freemen, their wives and children get the best spot – near the church
- then come the thralls and their families, further from the church
- lastly come the corpses washed ashore – so long as the corpse had a Norwegian hair-style. If it didn't then it was a foreigner – and it probably didn't get into the graveyard at all.

Did you know . . . ?
It was against the law to call a free-born man a "thrall" (a slave). The biggest disgrace was to die in a fight with a thrall.

Icelandic houses

Children and women would spend more time at home than the men. This must have been especially hard if you lived in a Viking house in Iceland . . .

To keep out the cold the Vikings lived in houses built of turf. The walls were thick and the houses looked like little hills. The children could play on the roofs . . . and keep the animals off, because the danger was that a hungry cow would climb up and eat through your roof.

The houses were pretty air-tight. The good news was that this kept out the cold. The bad news was that it also kept out the light and kept in the smoke from your fire. As your fuel may have been cattle-droppings then you had a choice – freeze outside or choke inside!

If you wanted a bath then you'd pop down to the bath house. It was what we'd call a "sauna" today. Water was poured over hot stones and you had a steam-clean. To really freshen up you'd whip yourself with twigs . . . then run outside to roll in the snow. If you were a softie then you'd go along to one of Iceland's warm-water springs.

78

Viking fun

Of course, there were no schools. Children learned by working alongside their mothers and fathers. But there would be a little time for play. If you'd like to try a Viking game, then play . . .

Kingy bats

1 Take a circle of wood about 40 cm across.
2 Glue or staple a strap across the back so you can hold it like a shield. Each player needs one of these bats.
3 Make a ball out of rags bound up with string (about the size of a tennis ball).
4 Stand in a circle and pass the rag ball.
5 To make it a competition, split into pairs. The winners are the pair who can keep the ball in the air longest without letting it hit the ground.

- Other children's games included making up poems and riddles. An adult game, which children might have tried, included a type of chess.

  And just as we have the shot put in today's athletics, the Vikings threw boulders. The furthest was the winner.

HE'S STRONGER THAN HE LOOKS

- Vikings made skates for crossing frozen rivers. The skates were made from bones, and poles were used to push the skaters along, rather like skiing today. The Vikings called their skates "ice-legs"!

A Viking game you probably wouldn't want to play: P-pick up a Puffin

In Iceland today, a Viking descendant describes the national sports as gannet-egg-gathering and puffin hunting. They catch flying puffins in a net on the end of a pole then wring their necks and eat them roasted. 12,000 puffins a year die like this.

So now you know something about life for Viking warriors, women and children. Now amaze your friends, your parents and even your horrible history teachers with . . .

Ten things you didn't know about the Vikings

1 Early Vikings had no buttons – they used brooches. And their houses had no windows.

2 The Viking blacksmiths hardened their swords by cooling them quickly in water – or sometimes in blood!

3 The children's song, *London Bridge is Falling Down*, is about a Viking attack led by Olaf. English soldiers fired arrows from the bridge into Olaf's attacking longboats. So Olaf attached ropes to the bridge's wooden legs and the other ends to his ships. The Vikings rowed away as fast as they could. Result . . . London Bridge was falling down!

4 If you made a sacrifice to the gods and wanted all your neighbours to know how good you were, then you'd put it on poles outside your front door!

WE COULD ONLY AFFORD A LEMMING THIS WEEK

5 Viking warriors could make close friends into "blood brothers" by cutting themselves and letting their blood mix. They often did the mixing under a circle of turf that had been lifted from the ground. Their blood mixed with the soil to make mud!

6 The Vikings made a promise by swearing an oath on a holy ring. This was a ring that was placed on an altar and reddened with the blood of a sacrificed animal.

7 One group of Vikings were reported to have a curious funeral custom. They split the dead man's possessions up and placed them in five or six portions. They placed these within a mile of the dead man's house. Then the men took their horses and raced to the piles. The first to get there won the dead man's loot!

8 The Vikings rarely took prisoners in sea battles because there was no room for them in the longboats. They let the losers drown or killed them.

9 No one was taken on board a longboat unless they had proved they were skilled with an oar, a sword and an axe.

10 Vikings shared their treasures evenly. You agreed what your share would be when you joined the longboat crew.

VILE VIKING FOOD

Would you like to eat a "cauldron snake"? Probably. It's the Viking name for a sausage spiced with thyme and garlic.

Summers were often short, cold and wet (just like Britain really!), whilst in winter it snowed from October to February. Crops had little time to grow, and poor harvests meant no food. So Vikings either starved or . . . went hunting.

Vile Viking joke:

Viking food you might like to try . . .

Some of the food, like cheeses and smoked meats, needed no cooking. Bread was baked and meat roasted on a spit, or baked in a deep pit covered with hot stones. Sometimes it was boiled in an iron cauldron.

Food and soup was served in wooden bowls, and drink taken from cups made from the horns of animals such as reindeer. The Vikings used knives, fingers and sometimes very small spoons – but no forks.

RECIPE FOR VIKING FISH SOUP

Ingredients:
The head of a large fish   Pepper
1 small haddock   Flour
Salt   Milk

Method:
1. Wash the fish head and haddock
2. Put them in a pan with 1 litre of cold water
3. Add 2 teaspoons of salt
4. Boil the water and skim the froth off the top
5. Add pepper and leave to simmer (boil gently) for 40 minutes
6. Strain the mixture to get rid of the bones and put the liquid (fish stock) back in the pan
7. Mix 2 tablespoons of flour with a cup of milk
8. Add the flour and milk mixture to the fish stock
9. Boil until the soup thickens
10. Check if it needs more salt or pepper
11. Serve with warm bread rolls

Some Viking foods you wouldn't want to try . . .

True or False? The Vikings ate . . .

1 Easily netted and very tasty in Viking stew

2 Nothing wasted, goose feathers were also used for bedding and quilts

3 A great alternative to chicken and goose

4 Skins used for clothing

5 A wild version of today's pig

6 Meat was eaten and the fur made into clothes or used for trade with other countries

7 Waste not want not. Walrus ivory was in great demand from those in foreign countries

8 Roaming through massive forests by the fjords, even moose weren't safe from the Vikings' bows. Their antlers were used as knife handles and hair combs

9 The Vikings appear to have been the first whale hunters. It often took between 10 and 15 men to kill just one whale, all taking turns to spear the poor creature. A long and painful death for the whale, but to the Vikings the whale was the scourge of the sea, often overturning their ships, so it deserved to die

10 Even the horses didn't escape the mighty Viking sword . . . yes, once the poor family nag was past it – chop!

The Vikings also enjoyed seaweed . . . the Welsh still eat it (but they call it lava bread) and it's considered a delicacy in Japanese restaurants.

During bad winters (most winters!) the Vikings ate anything they could catch, including foxes and ravens.

A Viking you wouldn't want to have tea with . . .

Harthacnut was Viking King of England from 1040 till 1042. He *could* have had a feast set out just once a day. If guests got hungry later, they *could* have eaten the leftovers. But Harthacnut wouldn't have this. When the guests had finished a feast he had the tables cleared of leftovers. Then another feast was set out. And after that another!

Every day he had FOUR feasts set out. Surprise, surprise – Harthacnut died young from eating and drinking too much.

What did Vikings drink?

Beer and mead were drunk from the horns of cattle. This was an art in itself – a trickle could soon become a tidal wave if the horn was tipped too far!

Another major problem was the horn's shape – it couldn't be put down unless it was empty. The drink had to be drunk in one go, hence a drunken Viking was a common sight.

Viking bread ... or, teeth don't grow on trees!

When food was scarce, Viking women made bread with flour, peas and pine-tree bark (for roughage and for vitamin C).

This, as you would imagine, would not taste very nice at all. It would be extremely heavy and filling and would most probably fall to the pit of your stomach – like a rock – AND it had rocks in it too! Experts have found small pieces of grit in samples of this bread taken from old Viking settlements in York.

Vicious Viking ancient joke:

VICIOUS VIKING HISTORIANS

We have learned a lot about the Vikings from the people who wrote histories of Britain many years ago. The trouble is that the writers often gave their opinions, which is not the same as giving us *facts*.

What they said about the Vikings . . .

> *For nearly 350 years we and our forebears have lived in this most lovely land. Never before has such a terror appeared in Britain as we have now suffered from this pagan race. No one thought such an attack could come from the sea.*

Alcuin 735–804 AD
— a monk and a very bad loser

> *The town of Hedeby (in Denmark) is poor in goods and wealth. The people's chief food is fish because there is so much of it. If a child is born there it is thrown into the sea to save bringing it up. I have never heard anything more horrible than their singing. It is more like the barking of dogs only twice as beastly.*

Al-Tartushi
— an Arab trader and a bit of a snob

. . . And what they didn't say!

> *A furore Normannorum, libera nos Domine.*
> (From the fury of the Northmen, deliver us, O Lord.)

This is what the poor English were *supposed* to have chanted as they trembled in their tiny churches. Nearly every book on the Vikings quotes this prayer of terrified people. The truth is there is no evidence that anyone ever actually said these words! It's simply something that scholars and teachers think they should have said.

What the Vikings did do . . .

There is a story that King Canute (or Knut) sat at the edge of the sea and tried to tell the tide to go back, saying "I command you not to rise over my land and not to wet the clothes or feet of your lord!" The tide came in anyway and soaked him.

The story is true. Teachers used to tell it to children and say, "What a foolish man King Canute was, children!"

BUT they forgot to say that the story went on – King Knut jumped back on dry land and said, "Let it be known to all people that the power of kings is empty and weak. Only one person is fit to be called king. That is the Lord God who is obeyed by heaven, by earth and by the sea!"

Knut took his golden crown off and never wore it again. He wasn't saying, "Look how great I am." He was saying, "Look how weak we are compared to God."

91

. . . and what they didn't do!

Samuel Pepys wrote in his diary of 10 April 1661 that he went

> *to Rochester and saw the cathedral where the great doors of the church are, they say, covered with the skins of the Danes.*

This was said to be the fate of invaders who were caught – skinned alive in revenge and the skin nailed to the church door. But tests on a "Daneskin" at Westminster Abbey proved it to be the skin of a cow!

Rotten Riddle

True or false . . . ?

1 There was a rule to stop Vikings fighting each other on the longboats.

2 King Alfred had a beard.

3 The Viking men and women wore make-up.

4 King Alfred's wife claimed that the god, Odin, was her ancestor.

5 Viking Halfdan was so wicked that God turned him mad and made him smell so rotten that no one would go near him.

6 The Viking longboats were as long as a tennis court.

7 A longboat sail could cover a tennis court.

8 The Saxon cure for losing your voice was to make the sign of the cross under your tongue.

9 Alfred the Great didn't build many monasteries because they were favourite targets of the Vikings.

10 Viking longboats had no seats.

Answers:
1 True 2 False 3 True 4 True 5 True (According to the monk, Simeon of Durham) 6 True 7 False (It would take three sails to cover a tennis court) 8 True 9 True 10 True (The oarsmen sat on the chests that carried their belongings)

THE SAVAGE SAXONS

The Vikings may have been called vicious but we have to remember they lived in harsh times. Their enemies in the British Isles, the Saxons, weren't far behind when it came to being cruel.

At least two English princes killed their brothers to win the throne of England: Harold Godwinsson did it through battle and Ethelred did it through murder. And they weren't the worst!

Six savage Saxon stories

1 King Edmund Ironside was a fierce fighter. In one battle, an enemy called Edric climbed a hill and waved a severed head in the air. "Surrender!" he called to Edmund's men. "This is the head of your leader, Edmund!"

Edmund was furious. He tore off his helmet to show his men that he was still alive. He then flung his spear at Edric. He threw it so hard that it bounced off Edric's shield and went through TWO soldiers who were standing beside him!

2 Edric's son finished Edmund off in the nastiest way you could imagine. One night Edmund went to a room with a pit that was used for a toilet. In the darkness he didn't see Edric's son hiding in the pit. As King Edmund sat down on the toilet the young man struck him twice from beneath with a dagger . . . ouch!

But the Viking King Knut was not amused by this cheating. When Edric went to tell Knut he'd got rid of the Vikings' greatest enemy he promised to reward Edric. "I will place you higher than any other English noble." He did. He cut off Edric's head and stuck it on the highest battlement of the Tower of London!

3 Earl Godwin was banished from England for disobeying the good King Edward. A year later Godwin returned. He went to dinner with the king and tried to be a bit of a creep. "People say I killed your brother," he told the king. "But, if that is true, then may God let this piece of bread choke me." A minute later Godwin was dead. He had choked on the piece of bread!

4 The Saxons were Christians and when they defeated the Vikings in battle they often made the Vikings become Christian. But Christianity at that time wasn't all sweetness and light! Early in the tenth century AD, Pope Stephen VI was elected as head of the Catholic Church in Rome. One of his first acts was to put the previous Pope, Formosus, on trial for dishonesty and evil living. Formosus was found guilty because he refused to plead when asked, "Are you guilty or not guilty?" Of course the reason he didn't plead was that he was dead at the time; Stephen VI had had him dug up and his body brought to court. The guilty corpse was thrown into the River Tiber. (You'll be pleased to hear that gruesome Stephen VI died soon after – imprisoned then strangled in his cell.) And they called the Vikings savages!

5 The Vikings attacked the north-east coast of England and its monasteries in 793 AD. Then, as your teacher and your timeline will tell you, they didn't bother much for another 40 years! Why not? The truth is too horrible for school books to tell you . . . but this *Horrible History* will tell you! After the 793 raid on Lindisfarne, the Vikings came back to attack the Jarrow monastery on the River Tyne. But this time bad weather held up their landing. By the time they reached the shore the local people were armed and ready. The Vikings landed – and were attacked fiercely. The Viking king was captured and tortured to death. The bloody remains were sent back to Denmark as a warning of what would happen if they tried to attack again! So the Vikings missed out England for 40 years . . . and went round to pillage Ireland instead!

6 The Saxons didn't like Abbot John of Athelney, even though he was King Alfred's choice. Abbot John was a German who was very harsh with the people who visited his churches. So the local people planned to kill him and dump his body outside the house of a woman. (They wanted it to look as if he was visiting her when he was killed by a jealous lover.) But the plot went wrong. The big abbot fought for his life. He was cut on the head but his cries brought help to rescue him.

Edmund's evil end

If King Edmund's serving girls could write, and if one of them had kept a diary, then some of it might have looked like this . . .

Ethel's Diary

27 May 946

Dear Diary,

That's it. I am packing this rotten job in. My mum wanted me to be a servant to the King. "A great honour," she said. "You start tomorrow!"

"That Edmund's a terrible man for chasing girls!" I told her. "Everybody's heard the story about him and that nun."

"Wulfhilda?" said Mum.

"That's the one. Had her taken to a convent in Hampshire so he could chat her up, didn't he?" I said.

"But he didn't," my mum pointed out.

"Only because she climbed down the convent drainpipes to escape! I don't want to go getting chased down drainpipes," I sniffed.

NOW WHERE'S SHE GONE?

Mum sighed. "King Edmund only chases after pretty girls. You'll be all right."

"Thanks mum," I snapped.

And mum went on to tell me about how to serve and clean and curtsey. She warned me not to spit or swear.

But she didn't warn me about the mess!

I mean to say, it's bad enough normally. All that

feasting and throwing bones on the floor. And that bad-tempered King Edmund ordering you about. But last night was the end . . . the end for Edmund and for me.

Blood all over the place!

It all started all right. These parties always do. The feast of St Augustine, of course, but that was just the excuse for a booze-up.

I was rushed off me feet all night. I didn't mind too much. They were good lads, mostly, as long as I kept their mead cups full. But there was one I didn't like the look of at all. Dirty hair over a low forehead and a scowl that could kill a cat.

Suddenly the King looks at this villain. He jumps to his feet and shouts, "Leofa!"

The ugly man rose to his feet and sneered. "That's me!"

"I banished you for thieving six years ago!" the King cried and rushed forward. He grabbed this Leofa by the hair – personally, I don't know how he could bear to touch that filthy mop. But he did, and he threw the robber on to the floor.

Now everyone gathered round in a circle and started shouting. You know the kind of thing, "Get stuck in, Eddie! Put the boot in, your highness!" and so on.

So the two of them are wrestling on the floor and suddenly the King gives a great cry. He jerks up and falls back.

I knew at once there was something wrong. I could tell because there was a long dagger sticking out of the king's chest.

"Ooooh!" the crowd gasped, as they do. All I could think was that all that blood would take a lot of clearing up in the morning.

And somebody yelled, "That's cheating, that is. Using daggers isn't fighting fair!"

And someone else said, "The King's dead . . . there'll be trouble, you mark my words."

Then a man behind me growled. "That's murder, that is! Get him, lads!"

Now I saw this with my own eyes so I swear it's true. Nobody used a weapon on Leofa. But in the flutter of a butterfly's wing Leofa was torn apart. That's right, torn.

It was a nasty death . . . but a quick one.

It was also a very messy one.

Oh, yes, they took the King's body away to give him a fine funeral. A lot of weeping and moaning and sadness. Very sad, I'm sure. But who gets the nasty job of clearing up that mess?

That's right. Me.

Well, I've had enough.

It might be a great honour to serve the King. But if they're going to go tearing people apart then I'm packing it in.

St Dunstan predicted the messy murder of Edmund. In a vision, he saw a devil dancing before him. It's a pity he didn't tell Edmund – the King could have worn his knife-proof vest. At least the nuns of Wessex felt a little safer after Edmund's murder! And young Wulfhilda became a saint.

THE SUFFERING SAXONS

Life in the Dark Ages was tough for the Saxons. They had more problems than simply vicious Viking raids to cope with . . .

Test your friends . . .

1 Saint Dunstan was on his way to the dying King Eadred when an angel appeared and announced, "Behold! King Eadred is departed in peace." But what did Dunstan's horse do?
a) Learned to speak and said, "Nay! Do not say so!"
b) Ran off and dumped Dunstan on his head

BLIMEY A TALKING HORSE.

BONCE

c) Dropped dead with shock at the sight of a dirty great angel

I OFTEN HAVE THIS EFFECT ON ANIMALS

2 The story of the Battle of Hastings is told in pictures on the Bayeux Tapestry. But what exactly is the Bayeux Tapestry?
a) A painting on cloth
b) A tapestry (that's a picture made by weaving threads)
c) An embroidery (a picture made by stitching)

3 The baby Ethelred was taken to church to be christened. The monk, St Dunstan, held the baby over the stone bowl that held the christening water – the font. Suddenly St Dunstan announced, "This is an evil sign! While this baby becomes king there will be death for many Saxons!" But what was the evil sign?

a) Lightning struck the church

b) Baby Ethelred cried all the way through the service

c) Baby Ethelred had a pee in the font

4 The Viking King Knut had a son who became king. His name was Harold Harefoot. A Saxon prince, Alfred, came to England to visit his mother. Harold Harefoot was worried that Alfred might try to take over the throne. What did horrible Harold do to Alfred's friends?

a) Locked them up in chains
b) Sold them as slaves
c) Scalped them

5 What did Harold do to Alfred himself?

a) Had his eyes put out
b) Made him promise not to lead a rebellion
c) Gave him money to go away

6 Harold Harefoot died in 1040 and his even-horribler-half-brother, Harthacnut, became king. What was his first act as king?

a) He had a statue built to honour his dear, dead brother, Harold

b) He had Harold dug up and buried in a specially-built church

c) He had Harold dug up, the head cut off and thrown into the Thames

7 King Harold Godwinsson was killed at the Battle of Hastings in 1066. But how did he die?

a) He was cut down by   **b)** He was hit in the eye
a knight's sword   with an arrow

c) He was wounded in the eye with an arrow then killed with a sword

8 King Alfred was buried in Hyde Abbey. But when Henry VIII abolished the abbeys, Alfred's bones were dug up. Eventually they ended up in Winchester Cathedral. What state are they in today?

a) Mixed up with the bones of other dead Saxons

b) Buried in their own grave

c) Cremated and the ashes scattered over the Edington battlefield

9 What cure would a Saxon doctor offer you for a bad stomach?

a) Drink a bowl of cat's milk mixed with a drop of dog's blood

b) Starve until noon, take a hot bath then drink treacle in warm water

c) Two indigestion tablets

10 Three Irish monks fled from the Vikings. They reached England safely. King Alfred saw this as a miracle of God because . . .

a) They had sailed in a boat made of wickerwork and stretched skins and had no food, no oars and no steering plank

b) They had walked across the Irish Sea at low tide

c) They had stolen a Viking longboat and sailed across the Irish Sea

8a) 9b) 10a)

Answers: 1c) 2c) 3c) 4a) b) and c) 5a) 6c) 7c)

104

Here's why!

1c) And, would you believe it, when Dunstan arrived at the palace, King Eadred was dead! He died at the moment that the angel appeared. (But he might have been able to save the king if his horse hadn't turned up its hooves and made Dunstan late!)

2c) It is a strip of embroidered linen measuring 40 metres by 50 centimetres – it tells the story a bit like a strip cartoon.

3c) Sure enough Ethelred was an unlucky king for the Saxons. Nearly as unlucky as the next baby to be christened in that font!

4a), b) and c) He also tortured and murdered some.

5a) The blinded Prince Alfred was handed over to a monastery and he spent the rest of his life with the monks.

6c) The dead Harold's head was dragged up in a fisherman's net and buried in the Danes' cemetery in London (St Clement Danes).

7c) That is the way Henry of Huntingdon described Harold's death. Some people have said the Bayeux tapestry shows Harold killed by an arrow, but it's not really clear. Harold's leg was hacked off after he was killed. William the Conqueror was so upset by this disgraceful act that he sacked the knight who did it.

105

The wicked woman of Wessex

In the nineteenth and twentieth centuries we've had more years when we were ruled by queens than by kings. But in the 300 years of Viking England there wasn't a single queen to be seen. Saxons reckoned this was because of one woman ruler who'd been so bad they never wanted another.

If there'd been a poet to tell her dreadful story then the poem would not have sounded like this! (Only the facts are right!)

Queen Eadburgh and Beothric

King Beothric married a woman, Eadburgh,
A bossy and vicious old crow.
He had a young pal that he liked quite a lot,
Till Eadburgh said, "He'll have to go!"

The King he refused and Eadburgh got cross,
So she poisoned poor Beothric's friend.
Alas for the King he had drunk the same stuff
And came to the same sticky end.

The Saxons they drove out the murdering fiend
And she fled with the loot from their house.
She went overseas to an Emperor's court
'Cos she wanted another rich spouse.

The Emperor said, "You may marry your choice.
Would you prefer me or my son?"
She picked the young prince and that made the dad
    mad!
He said, "Right then! You'll get neither one!"

Eadburgh was sent to a convent so quiet,
A house full of nuns good and dear.
But her parties and rave-ups became far too wild
So the nuns threw her out on her ear.

She wandered around with one servant and sank
Down to begging on streets, what a plight!
And that's how Eadburgh came to her sad end.
And the Saxons said, "Serves the bat right!"

KING ALFRED THE CAKE

King Alfred the Great was a winner
A true man of God, not a sinner,
He wrote several books
But wasn't a cook
So don't ask him to look after dinner!

King Alfred is the only king in English history to be called "Great". Just when it looked as if England was going to be overrun by Vikings, he led the resistance and saved at least half of the country.

Like many of the characters who lived in those days, the truth about his life is a little bit mixed up with stories. The trouble is that most of the stories come from a monk called Asser. Asser got his facts from Alfred . . . but Alfred could have told a few fibs to make himself look a great hero. Here are . . .

Tall stories about Alfred the Great

How many of these stories do you believe?

Story 1: Alfred the clever

As a five-year-old boy, Alfie was a bit of a cheat. His mother promised her sons that the first boy who could read her book would be given it. So Alf took it to a teacher. The teacher read it. Alf learned it off by heart, went back to his mum and recited it.

Facts: This is one of Asser's stories. In another part of his book Asser says Alfred couldn't read "until the twelfth year of his age or even more".

Story 2: Alfred the spy

He was also a bit of a cheat in later years. He dressed up as a minstrel, wandered into the Viking camp and listened to the Viking plans. A few days later he wandered back to the Saxon camp, spilled the beans, and battered the Vikings.

Facts: This is a story first written down 500 years after Alfred died. Would a king really risk his life in this way? The Vikings might not have recognised him as Alf – but they could have executed him anyway as a Saxon spy!

Story 3: Alfred the friend of a ghost

Alfred seems to have had a bit of supernatural help. The Saxons claimed that the ghost of St Cuthbert appeared to Alfred and told him how to beat the Vikings! After Alfred died he was buried in the old Hyde abbey until the building of Winchester was finished. Then he was moved. But monks claimed that his ghost stayed and haunted Hyde Abbey!

Facts: Asser said it was St Neot who appeared! But perhaps Asser was trying to show how great the south-of-England Saint, Neot, was. The Cuthbert story was told by a northern monk ... trying to prove how powerful the northern St Cuthbert was!

Story 4: Alfred the inventor 1

Alfred was supposed to have invented the clock! He needed to measure time so he could spend half of each day and night praying. But sundials don't work on cloudy days ... and they work even worse at night! So Alfred had candles marked in inches and measured the hours by the time it took to burn. But, in the draughty churches, the candles blew out. So ...

Story 5: Alfred the inventor 2

Alfred invented the lantern! There was no glass but clever Alf had ox-horn cut so thin that you could see clean through it.

Facts: Both are stories from Asser.

Story 6: Alfred the inventor 3

Alfred invented the navy. He decided that it was a good idea to attack the Vikings at sea, before they landed. At sea the Vikings were cramped into their longboats and couldn't fight and row at the same time. Great idea ... Alf made it work well.

Facts: The truth is his dad and his grandad both attacked the Vikings at sea as long ago as 851, off the Kent coast.

Story 7: Alfred the religious

Apart from praying day and night Alfred sent money to the Pope in Rome. In 883 Pope Marinus sent Alfred a present – a lump of wood that was supposed to be from the cross on which Jesus was crucified.

Facts: Marinus died. The next Pope, Formosus, pinched the church's money, and poisoned his brother and his wife. Alfred stopped sending money!

MAYBE IF I SENT ALFRED SOME MORE BITS OF WOOD HE'D START SENDING MONEY AGAIN

Story 8: Alfred the humble

When Alfred was having a bad time against the Viking invaders he hid out in a forest. A forester's wife gave him the job of watching her cakes to make sure they didn't burn. Alf was so busy fixing his bow that he forgot to turn the cakes over. They burned. The woman gave Alfred a piece of her mind. He could have said, "You can't talk to me like that – I'm the King!" Instead he just said, "Sorry."

Facts: This story is first found written down 400 years after it happened. Another 400 years passed and the Archbishop of Canterbury made a copy of Asser's book . . . and slipped the story of the burning cakes in! Other historians copied it, thinking it came from Asser and must be true!

Final Fact: Don't believe everything you read!!!

Judge for yourself

King Alfred took all the old laws and organised them into a new book of laws for the Saxons. Some of the laws were fair – others were pretty daft.

For example, there were four ways of finding out if a person was guilty of a crime. They were called ordeals. If you passed through the ordeal you were innocent – but if you failed you suffered from both the test and then a punishment.

Imagine you have been accused of a terrible crime – somebody has let your teacher's bicycle tyres down! The finger of suspicion is pointing at you.

"I didn't do it!" you cry.

"I think you did!" the tyreless teacher trembles. "Take a trial by ordeal! If you refuse to take the test then you are guilty – take your pick of ordeals!"

Choose your ordeal

1   **Ordeal by cake:** A special cake is baked. Swear,

"If I did this crime then may this cake choke me!"

and eat the cake.
If you're guilty
then you choke on the cake
– if you're innocent you live.

112

2 Ordeal by cold water: You are tied hand and foot. A rope is placed around you and you are lowered into a pool. If you sink then you are innocent . . . and with a bit of luck you'll be hauled out before you drown. If you float then you are guilty. You'll be dragged out and punished. (This silly test was still being used in the seventeenth century to test people accused of being witches!)

IF THESE ARE THE TRIALS I'D HATE TO HAVE THE PUNISHMENTS

3 Ordeal by hot water: Plunge your bare arm into a pot of hot water and pull out a stone at the bottom of the pot. Your arm will then be bandaged for three days. At the end of three days the bandage will be taken off. If the arm is healed then you are innocent . . . but if there is still a scald then you are guilty and you will be punished.

113

4 Ordeal by hot metal: You have to grip a rod of hot iron in your hand and walk with it for a set distance. Again the hand is bandaged for three days. If it's healed you're innocent – if there's a burn on your hand you're guilty.

CAN I DO ORDEAL BY COLD WATER NOW?

(Personally I'd go for the cake! What about you?)

Alfred's laws were based on the idea that you shouldn't do something if you wouldn't like to have it done to you.

Some of Alfred's punishments were quite reasonable . . . but the Vikings quickly learned that he could be harsh on sea-raiders. In summer 896 Alfred's navy captured a lot of Viking raiders. They were taken to Winchester and hanged as pirates. Alfred had no more trouble with Viking raids after that!

Saxon judges were given a clear idea of what punishments to give for crimes. Can you . . .

Make the punishment fit the crime?

1 The punishment for witchcraft (having dealings with the Devil) was . . .
a) Having your head shaved
b) Having to go to church every day for a year
c) Death

2 The penalty for plotting against your lord was . . .
a) Having "traitor" tattooed on your forehead
b) Death
c) Having your toes cut off

HOW DO YOU SPELL TRAITOR?

TRAT

3 The penalty for stealing a hive of bees was . . .
a) A fine
b) To be covered in honey and stung to death by the bees
c) To be covered in honey and thrown into a bear's cage

GAD! I'M BEING LICKED TO DEATH

115

4 The penalty for killing a man accidentally by letting a tree you are cutting fall on him . . .
a) You are hung from the tree
b) You are burned on a fire made from the wood of the tree
c) You must give the tree to the family of the dead man

WAIT A MINUTE, THIS CAN'T BE RIGHT

5 The penalty if your dog attacks and kills another person . . .
a) A fine of six shillings for the first killing, 12 shillings for a second killing and 30 shillings if it kills three people
b) The dog's owner is executed
c) The dog is executed
6 The penalty for telling nasty lies about a person was . . .
a) Having to walk a mile on your knees to their house and say "Sorry"
b) Having to write a letter of apology and stick it to the church door
c) Having your tongue cut out

7 The fines for beating a freeman, blinding him or cutting his hair were . . .

a) Ten shillings, twenty shillings and six shillings

b) Twenty shillings, six shillings and ten shillings

c) Six shillings, ten shillings and twenty shillings

8 The fine for accidentally stabbing a man with your spear depended on . . .

a) The *angle* the spear went into him

b) How *deep* the spear went into him

c) How much blood the victim lost

9 The penalty for murder was . . .

a) Hanging

b) Paying a fine to the relatives of the dead person

c) Going to prison for 20 years

10 The fine for offences against women varied. It depended on how important the woman was. Generally the fine for an offence against a nun was . . .

a) The same as for an offence against an ordinary woman

b) Half

c) Double

117

Vicious Viking law

If you didn't like Alfred's Law you could always move over the border into Danish England (Danelaw) and live by their rules. But the Viking Danes could be every bit as brutal as the English . . .

Danelaw 1: Sixty sheep to show you're sorry

Eyjolf was clumsy. Probably the clumsiest Viking in town. Tripping over sleeping dogs, dropping his sword on his toe and spilling his mead down his trousers.

"Now look what you've done! Your clumsiness will be the death of you," his wife, Thora, warned him as he crushed a cat beneath his clumsy foot.

"I'm off to the horse fight," Eyjolf muttered, and he snatched up his sword by the wrong end.

"Ouch!" he cried.

"Now look what you've done. Leave it at home,"

Thora sighed, "or else you'll kill someone."

"A Viking without a sword is like . . . is like . . ."

". . . is like a Viking with a brain. Very rare," she sniffed and stirred the stew.

Eyjolf barged through the door and there was a splintering of wood. "Now look what you've done! It helps if you lift the latch," Thora snapped.

The man walked carefully down the street and reached the horse-fighting circle without even hurting a single living thing. It was too good to last.

The horse fight was exciting. Hooves flew and men roared. "I've got my money on the black one!" Eyjolf cried as the stallion reared on its hind legs and lashed out with its front ones. "Kill!" Eyjolf shouted. He copied the lashing leg of his horse . . . and landed a punch clean in the eye of Bjarni the Brutal.

"Ooops! Sorry!" Eyjolf gasped. "Now look what I've done! It was an accident!"

Bjarni's sore eye closed. The other eye looked menacingly at Eyjolf. "You know what this means, Eyjolf!"

"Er . . . no!" Eyjolf said.

Suddenly the Viking men had lost interest in the fighting horses.

"Kill him, Bjarni!" Ragnar the Ruthless growled.

"Yeah! Chop his clumsy hand off!" someone else put in.

"I've a good mind to," the black-eyed man murmured.

"Oh, come on, Bjarni. It was an accident!" Eyjolf whined.

"It was an insult. And the only way to avenge an insult is to fight to the death! You owe me a debt of honour. I will take your life," Bjarni roared and waved his sword in the air.

"How about if I give you a gift instead?"

"You think you can buy my honour!" Bjarni cried.

"It was just a thought," Eyjolf shrugged.

"How much?" Bjarni demanded.

"Er . . . how about thirty sheep?"

"Sixty."

"It's a deal," Eyjolf agreed with a sigh of relief. "I'll deliver them when they're brought in from the hills this autumn."

"I'll come to your farm to pick the best," Bjarni snarled and stamped off over the muddy field.

"That Bjarni's a great fighter," Eyjolf groaned when he reached home. "He'd have killed me, Thora!"

His wife scowled at him with a look like a poisoned polar bear. "And perhaps it would be better if he had. We only have sixty-one sheep, you fool. Now look what you've done! We'll have nothing to live on this winter! Go and fetch me the bark off a tree."

"What for?"

"For your dinner. That's all you'll be eating for the next six months!"

And Eyjolf's father, Thormod, was just as bad. "Sixty sheep! Sixty sheep! You must be mad!" he raged that autumn as the sheep were being counted.

"All right, dad, no need to go on about it! Here's Bjarni now, come to collect his payment."

"Here! Bjarni! What sort of Viking do you call yourself? Taking sixty sheep from my son!" Thormod screeched. "You have the guts of a water-weed. What's the matter? Scared in case the clumsy clown beats you? Viking law says clearly that a quarrel must be settled by a fight to the death!"

The furious Bjarni said nothing. He simply turned purple with rage and drew his sword.

"Now look what you've done," Eyjolf grumbled. He drew his sword . . . and dropped it on his foot. As he bent to pick it up Bjarni's sword swept down – Eyjolf's head rolled in the mud.

"Now look what you've done," Thora said with a sad shake of the head. "Ah, well, at least honour is satisfied. I guess that means I get to keep the sheep!"

Bjarni turned and walked away without a word. Thormod was speechless. And Eyjolf wasn't saying anything . . . ever again.

121

Danelaw 2: How to finish a fight

Fights were very popular in the courts of Denmark and Sweden. But if a man was beaten, and wanted to have his life spared, then he had to go through a harsh test. This is how to finish a Viking fight . . .

1 Play some music on a fiddle and a drum.

2 Bring a wild cow into the hall where the fight has taken place. (Spectators are often trampled to death at this point. Try not to be one of them or you'll miss all the fun.)

3 All the hair is shaved off the tail of the wild cow. (This is an even more dangerous job than being a spectator – don't volunteer to do it!)

4 The tail of the wild cow is covered with grease.

5 The victim puts on shoes which are also covered in grease.

6 The victim has to get hold of the wild cow's tail. (And by now it will be really wild – so would you be if someone shaved your tail!)

7 The cow is then lashed with a whip. (Just to make sure it's really, really wild!)

8 If the man can hang on to the cow whilst it charges about the hall he can keep the cow. He can also keep his life.

(**Please note:** It is recommended that you do not try to sort out school-yard fights using this Viking method. The RSPCA would not allow it!)

123

TEST YOUR TEACHER

After reading this book you should know a bit more about the Vikings and the Saxons. Now's your chance to shock and amaze the people who thought you were as stupid as you look . . .

Here's a quiz for anyone who thinks they know anything about Viking times . . . like a teacher. If they get more than nine out of ten they're doing pretty well.

1 Eilmer was a monk at Malmesbury Abbey and in 1030 went down in history for being the first man to cover 200 metres . . .

a) Underwater

b) Flying

c) Running in under 25 seconds wearing his habit

2 When a Viking died a long way from home what might his friends do?

a) Bury him where he died

b) Have monks boil his body till there were just bones left and carry them home in a box

c) Cut out his heart and carry that home for burial

CAN'T YOU WAIT TILL I'M DEAD?

3 Why did the god Odin have only one eye?

a) He lost one in a fight with a raven

b) He swapped one for a drink from the well of wisdom

c) He gave one to some starving people to eat – they mixed it with milk to make eyes-cream

MUM! MY DESSERT IS LOOKING AT ME!

4 What was a tree-smith?

a) A carpenter

b) A woodcutter

c) One of the Smith family who lived in a tree-house

5 Vikings used "kennings" or word-play. So a "horse of the waves" was a ship. What was "the sweat of the sword"?

a) Rust

b) Blood

c) The handle where the warrior placed his sweaty hand

6 One Viking called his most prized possession "Leg Biter". But what was "Leg Biter"?

a) His guard dog

b) His sword

c) His pet polar bear

7 Vikings brought a lot of their words to the English language. But what does the place-name, "Follifoot", mean?

a) Stupid place to build a castle (Folly Fort)

b) Place of the horse fight

c) Place where Earl Folli first set foot

8 Did Vikings wear horns on their helmets?
a) Sometimes . . . for important ceremonies
b) Always
c) Never

9 How did the Vikings know which direction to sail in when they were in the middle of an uncharted ocean?
a) They used a compass
b) They threw a raven into the air and saw which way it flew to land

c) They tossed a coin to decide

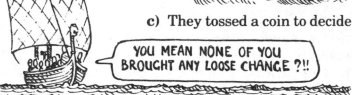

10 Where did the leader of a longboat crew sleep?
a) At the front of the ship to keep a lookout
b) In the middle of the ship so he was protected by men on all sides
c) At the back of the ship to be near the steersman

Here's how!

1b) Eilmer attached home-made wings to his arms and jumped off the top of the Abbey tower. After flying nearly 200 metres, the ground broke his fall. And he broke both legs and was crippled for life. He blamed his failure on the lack of a tail.

2b) A Professor Nylen believes that this explains why some graves are found with a jumble of bones rather than with them laid out correctly as if the body had been buried whole.

3b) If your teacher says the answer is c) then they're even dafter than they look!

4a) A "smith" was a craftsman. Vikings had weapon-smiths, ship-smiths, jewellery-smiths and so on.

5b) Blood was also known as the "sea of the wound".

6b) Swords were given names such as "Adder" . . . because its bite could kill. Another was known as "Gleam of Battle". What would you call yours?

10c) The second-in-command slept at the front.

EPILOGUE

Of course, this book has looked at the vicious side of Viking life. Not all the Vikings were vicious . . . and the ones who *were*, weren't vicious *all* the time. Some people even believe they were rather nice people. Good farmers, clever craftsmen and talented artists.

And some historians even argue that the Vikings were just *misunderstood*. They never really meant to invade England anyway! An early report of a Viking landing in Wessex describes a landing by just three ships. The local tax collector thought they were trying to do a bit of smuggling so he ordered them to be taken to the castle of the local king.

Afraid of being locked up, when all they wanted was to do a bit of trading, the Vikings killed the tax collector and his men. When they came back next time they brought their mates and decided to really teach those bossy English a lesson. That's how 300 years of misery for the English started.

But the historians who say the Vikings weren't vicious are kidding themselves. What they should say is the Vikings were no more vicious than the rest of the world at that time. Here are two final bits of horrible history. You make up your own mind.

The English king, Ethelred, wanted rid of all the Vikings in England – the farmers and traders who'd settled here, not just the warriors. On 13 November 1002 he ordered that all Danish people should be put to death. Many lost their lives, including Danish women, who were sometimes buried alive, and children. That was the vicious English for you.

Twelve years later a Viking army took hostages and demanded money and supplies for their men.

The Viking army was driven off by Ethelred's army. As they sailed home they stopped at Sandwich in Kent to drop off those hostages. The hostages were alive . . . but the Vikings had cut off their ears, their noses and their hands. That was the vicious Vikings. Who was worse? English or Viking?

The English king, Alfred the Great, was a strong and clever ruler who did a lot for the people of this island. But so was the Viking king, Knut the Great!

At 6 p.m. on Saturday 14 October 1066, the grandson of a Viking, King Harold Godwinsson, died at the Battle of Hastings. He was cut down by the sword of a Norman knight.

The Viking age was ended and the last Viking king was gone . . . or was he? Because, in a roundabout way, the vicious Vikings won in the end. First they conquered northern France, where a Viking was known as a North Man – or "Norman". Then the "Norman" William The Conqueror invaded Britain and won. So, if Normans are Vikings, then Vikings conquered England!

Nobody has ever invaded and conquered Britain since. If your family has lived in Britain since those times, it's certain that you have some Viking blood in you! Perhaps you may find out the next time you go to the zoo. If you find yourself looking at the polar bears, and feeling a strange urge to eat one . . .

130

THE MEASLY
MIDDLE AGES

With sincere thanks to Helen Greathead

Introduction

History is horrible. Horribly confusing at times. People can't even agree what happened yesterday . . .

When events happened last year, last century or hundreds of years ago we have no chance of knowing the whole truth . . .

You see the problem? Queen Isabeau was described as a tall, short, dark, fair woman, while French peasants were starving, well-fed, smelly people who had regular baths. Historians and teachers have usually said what they thought and that's not the same as giving the facts.

Who can you believe? No one! Your school-books will probably give you one side of the story . . .

This book will give you the other side . . .

Look at the facts and make up your own mind!

Timeline

410 The Romans in Britain go home. The Early Middle Ages start – usually known as the Dark Ages.

793 First Viking attack is on a monastery where the measly murderous maniacs massacre a few monks.

851 Vikings stay for the winter in England for the first time.

871 Alfred the Great becomes King of Wessex. He rules the south and kindly lets the Danish Vikings rule the north of England.

899 Alfred dead and buried. Alfred the Great becomes Alf-in-a-crate.

1017 Vikings triumph when Knut (or Canute) becomes king of all of England.

1066 Nutty Norman Knights aren't satisfied with living in France. The fighting fellers want Britain too. They invade, and hack English King Harold to bits. Their boss, William the Conker, pinches his throne. Historians usually start the Later Middle Ages here.

135

1086 Measly meanie William orders a record of all his land and people – so he can tax them. That's how the 'Domesday Book' came about.

1099 European armies set off to capture Jerusalem for the Christian Church. These religious expeditions to the Holy Land are known as Crusades. Away win for Crusaders!

1215 Measly King John gets too greedy for money and power. His barons make him sign the Magna Carta and give power back to the people . . . well, the rich people.

1264 Henry III has trouble with the barons. Rebel leader Simon de Montfort captures him and takes over the country for a year. The royal forces kill Simon within a year and send his head to Lady Mortimer as a gift. (And it wasn't even Christmas!)

1291 The Crusaders are driven out of the Holy land. End of Crusading. Who can these men in cans fight next? Each other!

1303 The Baltic Sea freezes over and starts what we now see as the Little Ice Age (lasts till 1700). Shorter growing seasons –

136

measly food means hunger and misery for millions.

1315 Floods compared to Noah's flood in the Bible. Ruined crops. Hungrier and miserabler millions. Reports from Europe of people eating cats, dogs, pigeons' droppings and even their own children.

1337 English king Edward III says he's king of France. The French don't agree and so they fight – and fight – and fight (on and off) . . . the start of the Hundred Years War.

1349 The Black Death kills off millions in Europe.

1431 French heroine Joan of Arc is captured after stuffing the English armies in battle. She is burned as a witch.

1453 Hundred Years War ends – 116 years after it started.

1459 Now the English start to fight each other! The Wars of the Roses between the Lancaster family (the red rose) and the York family (the white rose) for the throne of England.

1485 Henry Tudor wins the Battle of Bosworth Field and takes the crown from Richard III.

He unites the red and white roses.

1492 Christopher Columbus discovers America. New World, new age, end of measly Middle Ages (though nothing is ever quite that neat!).

Nasty Normans

The bruised Brits had been battered for a thousand years. In 43 AD the Romans ruined them, in the 5th century Saxons savaged them, in the 9th century the Vikings vanquished them. These were the Dark Ages. (No jokes about them being called 'Dark' because there were a lot of 'knights' around in those days.)

But in 1066 the Normans finally nobbled them. Even teachers know that William the Conqueror landed in 1066 and won the Battle of Hastings. The Nasty Normans took over.

These Normans were Vikings who'd settled in Northern France. They wore pointy hats. And who can blame them? They'd probably heard the story of King Geoffrey of Brittany . . .

King Geoffrey was on a journey to Rome when one of his hawks attacked a chicken in a tavern yard. The inn-keeper's wife was furious. She picked up a big iron pot and threw it at Geoff. It hit the king on the head and killed him. The nasty Normans nipped in and nicked Geoff's land for themselves – wearing helmets to avoid low-flying pots, of course.

The Normans had more writers and monks to record the history of their times. We are no longer 'in the dark' so much. We've left the Dark Ages and entered the Later Middle Ages.

The measly Middle Ages when times were tough and life was hard. Measly food and a measly death by plague . . . or war . . . or torture . . . or simply overwork.

And you think homework, school dinners and history lessons are bad?

Bloodthirsty Bill
Bill the Conqueror was Norman leader in 1066. He said King Edward of England had promised him the English throne – King Harold said the same thing. It was a fight to the death for two tough fellers. The English must have hoped Harold would win because Big Bill was bloodthirsty . . .

- William of Normandy was teased because he was said to be the son of a tanner – a leather-worker. When he attacked Alençon in France in 1048 the people poked fun at him by hanging out skins and shouting, 'Plenty of work for the tanner's son.' This may not have upset *you* – but it made Big Bill furious. He attacked and took 34

140

prisoners. He paraded them in front of the town walls. As the people of Alençon watched he had their hands and feet cut off and lobbed over the wall. 'That's what'll happen to you if you don't surrender,' he promised. They surrendered.

- William led an army against the Count of Arques. But he marched so fast that he arrived outside Arques town with just six men. The count was waiting with 300 knights. William charged at the Count who turned and galloped for the safety of the town. The 300 knights fled after him. And the Count was William's uncle!

- William wanted Maine in France as well as England. Walter of Mantes claimed both of them, too. Willy captured Wally and his wife and locked them up at Falaise where they died. Some historians say they were poisoned!

- When Will conquered England his reign was harsh. One historian of the time wrote that 'devils had come through the land with fire and sword'. But kind William abolished the death penalty. His last law said, 'I forbid that any man be executed or hanged for any offence, but let his eyes be gouged out.' Of course when an English earl called Waltheof rebelled in 1076 William *forgot* that law. Will gave Walt a chop at Winchester. Measly.

- Some English rebels didn't know how cruel William

could be. They soon found out in the North of England. When Will and his Normans marched on York every English man and boy they met was slaughtered. The army was broken up into smaller wrecking parties. Anything of any use to a human was destroyed – houses burned to the ground, crops burned, cattle killed and farm tools broken. From York to Durham a whole generation of people were wiped out. The roads were scattered with corpses and some said the survivors turned to cannibalism to stay alive. In 1086 York was still almost deserted.

You'll be pleased to know that when Billy the bully tried to do the same to a town called Mantes his horse trod on one of the burning cinders and stumbled. The fall hurt William's great gut and he died in agony.

Family feuds
The Normans didn't like the English – in fact they didn't even like their own family! William the Conqueror's brother, Odo, looked after England while Bill popped back

to Normandy. What thanks did Odo get? William threw him in jail!

But Bill's sons were worse. They fought against each other and they even fought against their dear old dad.

William the Conqueror probably couldn't write – he had clerks to do that for him. But if William could have written a letter to his wife Matilda in 1079 . . .

Gerberoi Castle
Normandy
January 1079

Dearest Matilda
        You won't believe what our Robert has gone and done! Only gone and beaten his dad in battle thats all! The ungrateful little swine (oops! Pardon my French.)
        As you know he was rebelling against my rule so I rode up to Gerberoi with a few hundred lads to sort him out. What does he do? He locks the gates. What do I do? Well, I besiege him don't I? A few hungry weeks without his venison pasties and he'll come begging for mercy, won't he. Always been fond of his grub has our Robert.
        But he doesn't! Instead he gets his forces together and comes charging out of the castle! He attacks me! I thought I was supposed to be attacking him!

Of course he's made a big mistake.
No one has ever beaten your William in battle as you know. He charges straight for me. Took me by surprise, that did. Knocked me clean off my horse. (Don't worry, my love, he didn't hurt me very much).

The rest of his men began moving in for the kill when that English lad, Toki, rides up with a fresh horse and saves my life. Poor young Toki got killed, but the main thing is I survived.

Now, I don't want to worry you, my darling, but our young Will was fighting on my side and he took a bit of a knock. He's recovering nicely and he's quite a hero. I always thought he was a useless little twerp until now, as you know. But I've decided to give him the throne of England when I go to that great throne in the sky.

As for Robert, he can have Normandy... and the ungrateful little beggar is welcome to it.

Home soon, my dearest one

William
(Conqueror)

Normandy
January 1079

Dear William

Just wait till I see our Robert. Fancy knocking you off your horse. He needs teaching some manners. Mind, I always did say you spoilt that boy something rotten. A few whacks with the flat of your sword would have done him no harm at all.

And I suppose you needed Toki's help because you are getting too fat to get back on your horse by yourself. When you get home you are going on a diet my lad.

Do you think you could remember to bring me some of that local woollen cloth? Green if you can get it.

Hurry home. The dogs are missing you, and I'm keeping your throne warm.

Love, Matilda

P.S. Don't forget to wipe your feet before you come into the great hall. I've just had new rushes put down.

William forgave Robert enough to leave him Normandy. But when old William died, young William Rufus got England. This caused a lot of quarrels between the brothers. Each wanted what the other had! A third brother, Henry, got just 5,000 pounds of silver. Who came off best?

Henry, actually.

William Rufus was killed by an arrow when he was out hunting in the New Forest – though some historians think measly Henry might have arranged that 'accident'. Henry took William's English throne, crossed over to Normandy and defeated Robert in battle and took Normandy too.

Henry had the lot. William the Conqueror would have been proud of his murdering, fighting, ruthless son!

The fatal forest
The story about William Rufus being shot in the New Forest is quite well known. His brother, Henry, is suspected of murder because he was in the same forest at the time of William's death.

But, strangest of all is the fate of Richard. Richard who? Richard was the fourth son of William the Conqueror. In 1074 Richard was killed in a riding accident . . . guess where? That's right – in the New Forest.

Richard came to a very painful end. He was charging through the forest on his horse when he collided with a tree. (There were no driving tests for horse riders in those days. If there had been then Richard would have failed.)

Richard was carried back to Winchester, but his injuries were so bad that he died soon after.

William the Conqueror was really upset. (And the tree can't have been too happy either!)

Feudal fellows

The Normans brought the 'feudal system' with them. The king was at the top of the heap and peasants at the bottom. They paid for everything – they worked in his fields, worked in his castle, repaired his roads . . . all for free. The peasant then worked on a small patch of his own land in his spare time – not a lot of *that*. If the peasant made any money then he paid taxes to his lord. He paid the lord for grinding his corn, pressing his apples or baking his bread in the measly lord's oven.

The feudal system

I'M A VILLEIN. MY LORD LETS ME LIVE ON HIS LAND. IN RETURN I WORK FOR HIM. I'M A SLAVE-THE LOWEST OF THE LOW

AND I'M EVEN LOWER THAN YOU

I'M A FREE PEASANT. I FARM THE LAND OWNED BY MY LORD. IN RETURN I PAY HIM RENT. I'M POOR AND MISERABLE

I'M POOR, MISERABLE *AND* OVERWORKED

I'M A KNIGHT. I GET MY LAND FROM THE KING. IN RETURN I FIGHT FOR HIM WHEN HE NEEDS ME. NOTHING BUT FIGHT, FIGHT, FIGHT.

AND WHO HAS TO LOOK AFTER THE LANDS WHILE HE'S AWAY? POOR ME!

And the plagues of the 14th century certainly changed the world. After the Black Death there weren't so many peasants about! Peasants became rare . . . and valuable!

You'd think the peasants would be better off dead – they weren't! After a peasant died the measly lord took his best possessions . . . after all they had only been 'loaned' to the peasant during his lifetime. No wonder . . .

The peasants are revolting

In the measly Middle Ages peasants had a short life, but a miserable one. If overwork didn't kill you then you could die from ordinary things like a rotten tooth. Storing food over the winter could give you a type of food poisoning. Then there were extra nice diseases to look forward to, like St Anthony's Fire – an arm or a leg would get a burning pain . . . then drop off.

When you died you'd hope to go to heaven, but stories went around that a peasant's soul didn't get to heaven – demons refused to carry it because of the horrible smell. They were *really* revolting!

While the peasants froze in the fields, died in ditches or starved in slums, the rich people had 'fun'. In the 14th century Count Robert of Artois had a very pleasant garden. It had . . .

● statues that squirted water at you as you walked past
● a trapdoor that dropped you on to a feather bed
● a hosepipe that squirted water up ladies' dresses
● a statue that squawked at you like a parrot
● a room that greeted you with a thunder storm as you opened the door

HAVE A NICE RELAXING WALK IN THE GARDEN HE SAID... HA, HA.

149

No wonder the peasants hated the nobles in their castles. The peasants didn't go to school but they knew one simple sum: 'There are more of US than there are of THEM!' In France in 1358 they decided to take over.

The French rebellion was known as the Jacquerie because . . .

1 Any peasant was known as a 'Jacques' (a 'John' in English) – a very common name – so it was a revolt of the 'Johns'! Or . . .

2 They wore padded, boiled-leather jackets as a sort of cheap armour and these jackets were called 'Jacques' – so it was a revolt of the padded-boiled-leather-jackets.

Take your pick. Either explanation could be right – or both could be wrong!

Of course the peasants weren't used to organizing themselves – the nobles were. At first the Jacques murdered a few surprised nobles . . .

22 June 1358 *The PARIS POST* STILL ONLY 25 CENTIMES

PEASANTS HAVE KNIGHTS IN DAZE!

The brave battling peasant army has a new leader who is leading the jolly Jacquerie to victory. His name is Will Cale and he's just what the proud peasants need – a strong leader and an experienced soldier.

The revolt began four weeks ago when the peasants grew furious that

150

the French king had been captured by the English and the noble knights had done nothing – except run away. Armed with axes, scythes and pitchforks a 10,000-strong army captured over a hundred castles.

Knights fled with their families – or stayed and died. There are reports of Jacques jokes like roasting a knight on a spit – then forcing his wife to eat the roasted flesh!

Amazingly, two enemies, an English knight and a French knight, joined forces to help Meaux when it suffered a Jacques attack. Captal de Buch and Gaston Phoebus said, 'When noble ladies are in danger a knight's gotta do what a knight's gotta do.'

The knights with an armed force of just 120 cut the Jacques to pieces with their weapons. 'Using swords against scythes is cheating,' Will Cale grumbled.

Now there are rumours that Charles of Navarre is leading a fightback in the east. Cool Cale says, 'Charles of Navarre? Charlie's for the chop – you'll see.'

The Paris Post supports their battling efforts.

Our Brave Boys

But Charles of Navarre used one weapon that Will Cale didn't have . . . brains!

22 July 1358

The PARIS POST

STILL ONLY 25 CENTIMES

CRUEL CALE CONQUERED

The knights are back in power – where they belong! The Paris Post proudly announces that Wicked Will Cale is dead. The Jacquerie is over! Peace has returned to our troubled towns.

Charles of Navarre's likeable lads faced Will Cale's revolting rats near Paris. Charles suggested that they should talk and Cale, the clot, arrived without a guard. Naturally, Navarre nabbed him and locked him in chains! 'That's cheating!' Cale cried but no one was listening. The leaderless louts of the Jacquerie were massacred – or ran like rabbits.

Cheerful Charles gave Cale the crown he craved – a crown of red hot iron! Then he cut off his hateful head. Now he plans to lead an army of destruction through the region. 'Peasant houses, fields and families will be destroyed!' the noble Navarre promised.

The Paris Post supports the overthrow of the sewer-scented masses and the return of our true leaders.

Champion Charlie

The English peasants were a little way behind the French when it came to rebelling. The English peasants' revolt happened 23 years later in 1381. It wasn't only the French knights who could do a bit of cheating. English King Richard II was pretty good at it too!

The peasants in southern England were so fed up with paying a Poll Tax that they marched on London to see the king. They murdered a few unpopular lords on the way and stuck their heads on long poles . . .

But the lords were probably glad to have their noses well away from the smelly marching feet!

The head of the revolting peasants was called Wat Tyler . . . which could have been a problem . . .

Anyway, Wat's 20,000 rebels reached London and presented their demands . . .

The lords in London promised to give in to his demands. Wat didn't believe them (what a wise Wat!). His army raised their trusty, rusty swords and marched into London, murdered a bishop, a lord or two and as many foreigners as they could get their scythes on. The 14-year-old king (Richard II) perched on a war horse promised Wat his support! Wat believed the king. (Showing he was really an unwise Wat.) The head peasant boasted . . .

In four days' time all the laws of England shall be coming from my mouth!

But Wat Tyler hadn't read his Horrible History books. He didn't learn from what had happened to Will Cale 23 years before. He agreed to meet the king and his guards at Smithfield.

Some historians say that Wat Tyler began by picking a fight with the king's squire and drew his knife. The Lord Mayor of London (William Walworth) drew his sword and killed Tyler.

The leaderless peasants gave in – just as the French peasants had after Cale's death.

Which just goes to show . . . history repeats itself . . . itself . . . itself . . . itself . . . itself . . . itself . . .

Wat's head was stuck on a lance. The head peasant had become a head-less peasant.

The Saxon streaker

William and his Normans are famous for the Domesday Book – a record of everything everyone owned in England. Once the Normans knew what people were worth then they could tax them. A lot of people forget that the poor people of England knew all about paying tax – long before the Normans arrived.

The most famous tax dodge was the deal made by a famous Saxon streaker called Lady Godiva. Roger of Wendover wrote the first report of her daring deed. Here it is in modern English. What is missing from Roger's version of this famous story?

The good Countess Godiva longed to free the town of Coventry from the misery of heavy taxes. She often begged her measly husband, Earl Leofric of Chester, to free the town of those taxes. The Earl laughed at her. 'Your request is foolish,' he said. 'Don't you see how we need that money? To cut those taxes would be to hurt me. Don't ever mention the subject again.'

WE HAVE A VERY EXPENSIVE LIFESTYLE

But Countess Godiva had the stubbornness of a woman (a very sexist remark that Wendover would not get away with today). She would not stop pestering her husband about the matter until finally he snapped at her, 'Get on your horse, ride naked through the market place in front of all the people. If you do that I shall grant your request.'

Countess Godiva replied, 'If I am willing to do this do I have your permission?'

'You do,' he agreed.

At this the Countess loosened her hair and let it fall until it covered her body like a veil. She mounted her horse and, escorted by two knights, she rode through the market place without being seen except for her fair legs.

When she had completed the journey she happily returned to her astonished husband and was granted her request. Earl Leofric freed the town of Coventry from all taxes.

When the story was repeated a hundred years later a historian added a new character to the story. A fiendish feller called Peeping Tom. While all the other citizens of Coventry went indoors and gave the Countess some privacy, terrible Tom spied on her.

Which just goes to show – don't believe every story you read . . . especially history stories!

Did you know . . . ?

A knight owned his peasants – they were considered part of his wealth. If you attacked a knight then he'd probably shut himself safely away in his castle. The next best thing to do was to attack his peasants in the villages around. In 12th-century France, Thomas de Marle (nickname 'The Raging Wolf') attacked his father's peasants, cut off their feet or put out their eyes. What a measly way to go!

Dreadful disease

In 1347 Death strolled through Europe with his scythe, mowing some down and missing others. Swish! Swish! In 1349 he sailed across the Channel to the British Isles. The terrified people never knew who was going to be next. As an Italian diary recorded . . .

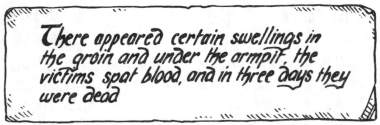

There appeared certain swellings in the groin and under the armpit, the victims spat blood, and in three days they were dead

These swellings began to ooze with blood and pus. Purple-black blotches appeared on the skin and you smelled absolutely revolting!

Swell - Spit - Smell - Swish! You were gone.

Death's 'scythe' was the bubonic plague and the piles of bodies grew like chopped straw into a haystack. They were loaded on to carts, dropped into pits – or, in Avignon in France, thrown in the river.

Children were Death's particular favourites when it came to the swish. We now know the real reason for this: if you are an adult then you have had quite a few diseases in your lifetime and build up a 'resistance'; children have had fewer diseases and far less resistance. They die easily.

Of course, preachers said the children probably got what they deserved! One explained . . .

It may be that children suffer heaven's revenge because they miss going to church or because they despise their fathers and mothers. God kills children with the plague – as you can see every day – because, according to the old law, children who are rebels (or disobedient to their parents) are punished by death.

You can see that not much has changed.

DO WHAT I SAY... OR DIE!

SWISH

159

Crazy cures

The trouble was that doctors didn't know what caused the plague and they didn't know how to cure it. People mistakenly believed you could catch it by . . .

- looking at a victim
- breathing bad air
- drinking from poisoned wells.

In France they said the English did the poisoning, in Spain they blamed the Arabs. In Germany, suspected poisoners were nailed into barrels and thrown into the river. And everyone blamed lepers!

And the cures were almost as dreadful as the disease. Doctors already had some wacky cures for illnesses. They said . . .

- wear a magpie's beak around the neck to cure toothache
- cut a hole in the skull to let out the devil and cure madness.

With something as deadly as the bubonic plague they had no chance! They suggested . . .

- throw sweet-smelling herbs on a fire to clean the air
- sit in a sewer so the bad air of the plague is driven off by the worse air of the drains

- drink a medicine of ten-year-old treacle
- swallow powders of crushed emeralds (for the rich)

- eat arsenic powder (highly poisonous!)
- try letting blood out of the patient (when the patient's horoscope was right!)
- kill all the cats and dogs in the town
- shave a live chicken's bottom and strap it to the plague sore

- march from town to town flogging yourself with a whip.

The doctors checked the urine of their patients. If there was blood in it then there was no hope.

Some people who caught the plague had a natural resistance to it so they recovered. Others took the only 'cure' that worked – run away from the plague-infested towns into the countryside. The rich people, with country houses, could do this. The poor stayed at home and died.

The real cause of the plague wasn't discovered till just a hundred years ago. And people still don't understand – they think rats carried the plague. Fleas carried the plague germs. They lived on rats and their germs killed the rats.

A dead rat is not very tasty (as children who stay to school dinners will tell you) so the fleas looked for a new 'home'. If there were no rats about then the fleas would hop on to a human and spread the germs to that human. When their new human friend died they'd hop on to another human – maybe the person who'd nursed the first victim. And so it went on.

Suffering Scots

The plague had its funny side – if you have that sort of sick sense of humour! The Scots hated the English and were delighted to see the plague destroying so many of their old enemy.

They decided 1349 would be a good time to invade – the English would be too weak to defend themselves. As their forces gathered the plague struck. Many Scots soldiers died – many more ran home to their towns and villages . . . taking the plague with them! In the wars between England and Scotland, Death didn't take sides.

Plague dogs

In Messina, on the Italian island of Sicily, people believed that plague death appeared as a large black dog. It carried a sword in its paws and smashed the ornaments and altars in their churches. Many swore they had seen it!

In Scandinavia the people saw Death as a Pest Maiden. She flew out of the mouths of the dead and drifted along in the form of a flame to infect the next house. (Never give the kiss of life to a plague victim or you'd get singed lips!)

In Lithuania a similar maiden waved a red scarf through the window to let in Death. A brave man saw the waving scarf and sliced off the maiden's hand. He died but the village was saved. The scarf was kept in the local church for many years. (Of course, it could have belonged to some 'armless girl, couldn't it?)

Fantastic flagellants

Some people believed the best way to get rid of your wickedness was to beat the devil out of you. In Europe groups of 200 to 300 people called flagellants went around whipping themselves (and each other) for 33.3 days – the number of years Christ lived on Earth. Apart from the steel-tipped whips, they had to put up with . . .

No shaving
No washing
No change of clothes
No comfortable bed
No talking to women

At first the flagellants blamed the priests for the evil of the plague. But the priests fought back with threats to ban the flagellants. So the measly flagellants decided to blame an easier target – the Jewish people in towns. They rushed to the Jewish part of each town and murdered everyone they could find.

In some places, like Worms (in Germany) in 1349, the Jewish people cheated the flagellants of their sport – they set fire to themselves in their houses in a mass suicide. Six thousand died in Mainz that year and not one of the 3,000 Jewish people in Erfurt survived.

Mystic medicine

Of course the Black Death was not the only illness that doctors had to deal with in the Middle Ages.

Since ancient times doctors believed that one of the best ways to get rid of sickness was to let the bad blood out of your body. People of the Middle Ages would pop down to the local barber shop and have a vein opened. (If you wanted to save time you could have your hair cut while you waited!)

How could you spot the local barber shop? There was usually a bowl of fresh blood in the window! (In London this was considered bleeding bad taste and banned in 1307. All blood had to be thrown straight into the Thames.)

Apart from bleeding there were other 'interesting' cures in the Middle Ages. But can you match the right cure to the right illness? Try this test – it doesn't matter if you get them all wrong, actually. None of them works anyway!

165

Answers:

1f) Washing in a boy's pee might kill you so it would certainly give your ringworm a nasty shock. (Don't try this at home.)

2i) Warning! Don't try to eat the honey after you've finished with it.

3a) Plague doctors sold powdered pearls or powdered emeralds to very rich parents. This was very healthy for the doctor's wallet.

4h) In the mid-14th century a vicar was caught importing four dead (and smelly) wolves' bodies in a barrel. The idea was that the disease would 'feed' on the wolf skin instead of the human sufferer. Surgeons were furious that a vicar was pinching their job!

5b) Eating ginger for loss of memory is quite harmless. I tried it once. It may even have worked – but I can't remember.

6e) Treacle was the great cure of the 15th century. It cured practically everything – including loss of speech, spotty skin and snake bites. (It was a real star among medicines, hence the song, 'Treacle, treacle little star, how I wonder what you are.')

7d) Bacon fat should be mixed with wild boar's grease if you can get it. The trouble is you'd probably get more bruises fighting the boar. Then you'd have to go out and catch another wild boar . . . and so on! Note: An angry teacher should not be killed for his or her grease. They are wild BORES, not boars.

8j) Make sure the feathers are not still attached to the chicken when you set fire to them. The RSPCA takes a very dim view of this.

9c) 'Snot a very nice cure, this one.

10g) If you are embarrassed by a dead toad hanging round your neck, tell your friends it's the latest fashion. Alternatively you may prefer to bleed to death.

Top tip for teachers

The best way to avoid a hangover is to drink with your hat off. Doctors of the Middle Ages said this allows the harmful fumes to pass out of your head. A hat holds them in and gives you a headache. But if the drink affects your kidneys then here's a beetle brew discovered by John of Gaddesden . . .

I cut off the heads and wings of crickets and put them with beetles and oil in a pot. I covered it and left it a day and a night in a bread oven. I drew out the pot and heated it at a moderate fire. I ground it all together and rubbed the sick parts. In three days the pain disappeared.

SPOING

(**Health warning**: Make sure you use crickets, or little grasshoppers, and not cricketers in this cure. Try cutting a cricketer's head off and you may get a bat in your measly mouth.)

Arab medicine

Arab doctors were far in advance of European doctors. Their cures showed more understanding of disease and

167

their treatments were more gentle – and usually more successful. They could scarcely believe the way doctors behaved in Europe.

Usama ibn Muniqidh told the story of an Arab doctor. He was treating a knight who had an abscess on his leg; he put a dressing on it. For a woman with a lung disease he prescribed the right sort of fresh food.

Along came a European doctor. 'You have no idea how to cure these people,' he said. First he took an axe and cut the knight's leg off. The knight died.

Then he cut a hole in the woman's skull, removed her brain and rubbed it with salt. The woman died.

'I hope you have learned something about medicine today,' the European doctor said.

'I certainly have,' the Arab doctor replied.

The first flying doctor

Australians are proud of their 'Flying Doctors' – a medical service in aeroplanes. But the Middle Ages saw Doctor Damien of Stirling in Scotland become the first doctor to take to the air.

Doctor Damien was a hopeless doctor and killed as many as he cured. Measly-brained King James IV gave him lots of money to turn ordinary metals into gold – but he failed. Then in 1504 he tried flying. A writer of the time said . . .

Damien took it in hand to fly with wings, so he made a pair of wings from feathers. These being fastened around him he flew from the walls of Stirling Castle, but soon fell to the ground and broke three bones. He blamed the failure on the fact that there were chicken feathers in the wings. He said, 'Chickens belong on a dung heap and not in the air.'

BOUNCE

Luckily King James was a pretty good doctor himself and could patch up Damien. The first flying doctor was no chicken – which is more than can be said for his wings!

Nutty knights

The Normans brought the art of castle-building to Britain. Mounds of earth with a wooden wall protected them from the beaten Brits. As they settled in, the castles became larger and were built of stone because now they were protecting themselves from each other!

Of course, castles weren't built by just any old peasant. They were built by knights. Wealthy and powerful soldiers who wore armour and fought on horse-back. These knights were big bullies who battered British peasants into doing as they were told or fought for the king and battered foreign peasants.

Then knights and kings began to do something disastrous . . . they learned how to read! Now they read stories about an ancient king called Arthur of Britain. And Arthur had a strange idea: knights should be gentlemen. Knights treated ladies with respect but, weirdest of all, they treated their enemies with respect! King Edward III (ruled 1327 till 1377) even created a Round Table just like King Arthur was supposed to have.

A knightly fight now had rules. You didn't sneak up on another knight and stab him in the back, even though that saves a lot of trouble and effort. You had to challenge your opponent to a fight and agree the time and place. This may seem a bit strange to you or me – it's like saying, 'Excuse me, my dear fellow, but would you meet me next Thursday, at noon at the meadow by the river, when I will do my best to beat your brains out?'

But, as the boy who put a drawing pin on the head-teacher's chair said, 'Rules are there to be broken.'

Forget the fairy-tales about knights in shining armour battling boldly to win glory . . . or death. In truly horrible historical fashion, the most measly knights of the Middle Ages broke the rules. They cheated.

This true 12th-century story is from Ludlow Castle on the border between England and Wales. We learn not all knights were gentlemen – not all maidens were meek and weak. And, in horrible history, not all stories have a happy ending . . .

Midnight terror (or, Terror amid knights)

'Women?' the young knight, Geoffrey, laughed and the sound echoed round the cold stone walls of the dungeon cell. 'They love me. And who can blame them. I'm handsome, strong and brave. Any woman would be proud to be my love!'

The rat twitched his whiskers and scuttled back to its

nest under the straw. 'You don't appear to believe me, Master Rat,' the young man said. 'I'll bet you a piece of stale bread that I'll be out of here within a week!'

Geoffrey turned his head sharply as he heard the rattle of keys in the lock of the cell. He brushed the straw off his jerkin, sat up straight and fixed a smile upon his face. The door swung open and the girl hurried in with a dish of gruel and a mug of ale. Her nose curled back at the smell in the filthy air and she placed the food carefully on the floor. It was the only time she would come within reach of the chained man. Suddenly his chain clattered, his hand shot out and grabbed her wrist.

'Ah!' she cried.

'Hush!' he said quickly. 'Stay just a few moments, Marian,' he went on softly.

'My father will be suspicious,' she said anxiously.

Geoffrey spoke quickly and didn't release his grip on the girl's wrist. 'Yesterday, after you'd gone, his lordship came to see me. He has given me just three days to talk. He wants me to tell him our plans for capturing Ludlow Castle. I would not betray my friends, of course.'

'And after three days?' she asked.

'After three days he will torture me. First he will use hot irons on my face . . .'

'No!' she gasped.

'I can bear the pain,' the young man shrugged, 'but it may spoil my looks. No maiden would marry me with those scars. Or he may gouge out my eyes . . .'

'No!' she gasped. 'His lordship's not a cruel man.'

The prisoner shrugged one shoulder. 'We'll see . . . at least *you'll* see. I won't have any eyes left to see!'

'How can you joke about such a thing?' she asked.

'True. I'd be sad to lose my eyes. I'd never be able to see a beautiful face again. A beautiful face like yours.'

The girl blushed and tore her wrist away from his grip. She hurried from the cell and closed the door. The young man smiled.

The next day she came in and knelt beside him silently. She took a small key from her belt and unfastened the chains that bound his wrists. She slipped a larger key from the ring and pressed it into his hand. 'The key to the outer door,' she muttered.

He touched her hand softly. 'Thank you, Marian. You have saved me and I owe you my life. The only way I can

173

repay my debt is by marrying you.'

The girl looked up, startled. 'You'll take me with you?'

'Ah!' he whispered. 'Not just yet. I need time to get away. I want you to stay here, to cover for my escape as long as you can. I'll return for you a week today. Listen, here's what we'll do . . .'

That night, as the monastery bell tolled midnight, he slipped away from the moon-shadows of the castle and stole a horse from the village below. Within an hour he was ten miles from Ludlow. Within a week he was back, as he had promised.

A ladder hung from the window as he knew it would. It was made of strong leather rope and led up to a window in the west tower. A window that wasn't overlooked by the patrolling guards.

Geoffrey climbed it swiftly and felt Marian's strong hands grasp his wrists and pull him over the stone sill. A candle lit the room and glinted on the knight's excited eyes. Marian gave him a nervous smile and moved towards the window. 'Where are you going?' he asked.

'Down the ladder. Away with you,' she said.

He shook his head. 'We have one or two visitors who want to climb that ladder first,' Geoffrey grinned.

'Visitors?'

'Friends of mine. Friends who want a little revenge on your lord.'

A man's face appeared at the window ledge. Geoffrey pulled him into the room. That man in turn helped a second then a third. In five minutes the room was crowded with hard-faced, leather-jacketed men with soft boots and cruel knives.

'What are you doing?' the bewildered girl asked.

Geoffrey ignored her. Instead he turned his back on her and spoke to the men. 'Kill the guards, throw their bodies over the walls then lower the drawbridge . . .'

'My father's on duty tonight!' Marian cried.

'Kill *all* the guards,' Geoffrey said slowly. 'Our troops will ride in and finish the job.'

Marian opened her mouth but before she could scream a warning the knight had clamped a rough, gloved hand over it. He held it suffocatingly tight until the last man had left the room and closed the door. 'Women are fools,' he sneered at her.

But while he held her mouth closed he couldn't control her arms. She had carefully slipped the dagger from his belt and turned it till the point was under his ribs. With all of her strength she pushed upwards.

His lips went tense and his eyes showed more surprise than pain. There was a soft gurgle in his throat as he fell back against the wall. He remained there for half a minute, clawing helplessly at the thing in his side before he slid slowly to the floor.

Marian hurried to the door and looked out on to the battlements. There were cries of terror as men struggled in the darkness and tumbled from their posts. The drawbridge dropped with a crash and there was the sound of horses clattering into the courtyard.

One man's voice seemed to rise above the other cries. 'We've been betrayed!' the voice wailed. 'Betrayed.'

Marian turned back to the room, walked past the lifeless knight and climbed on to the window ledge. 'Oh, we've all been betrayed,' she said dully. The girl simply leaned forward and let herself drop.

In the dark chaos of the night no one heard one more small cry, one more soft crunching of bone on rock.

Did you know . . . ?

Marian wasn't the only castle-dweller to be betrayed. A robber held in Haverfordwest in Wales became friends with some young squires who were training to be knights. He fixed arrowheads for them and gave them to the boys for their bows. The boys begged that the robber be allowed out for some fresh air – in their care. He took them hostage and used them to bargain for his freedom.

And Marian wasn't the only young woman to die in a fall from a castle. Just over the Welsh border in Abergavenny a young girl fell while trying to catch her pet squirrel that had escaped.

Jolly jesters

Castle life wasn't all dungeons, doom and draughts. There were feasts and entertainments. The chief entertainer was the jester.

A 13th-century writer described the skills a jester needed if he was going to get a job in a royal castle . . .

A jester's little joke

Jesters also had to be quick witted. At the Battle of Sluys (1340) the measly English archers fired so many arrows that the French were driven from the decks of the ships and their fleet destroyed. No one dared tell King Philip VI of France. His jester stepped forward . . .

Reports said that the fish drank so much French blood that if they could talk they would have spoken French!

A terrible tale

Jesters weren't the only entertainers in castles at the time. There were minstrels too. They had heroic tales of knights and dragons and ladies. Of course, they didn't have comics in the Middle Ages but they had cheerful little stories that would have made very good comic strips. Stories like 'Renault and the Dame of Fayel' . . .

179

Awful Angevins

King Stephen followed Henry I as the last Norman king. Henry Duke of Anjou wanted the English throne and, since he was a bit rough, no one argued with him – not even Stephen's sons.

When old Steve died, in 1154, Henry of Anjou became Henry II – the first Anjou (or Angevin) king. Henry had lots of bright ideas for improving England and one of the first things he sorted out was the law. Now . . .

- Accused people could be tried by the people of their own class – juries. (A bit like your classmates deciding if you are guilty of the crime of slopping your school-dinner custard down Alice Anderson's neck.)
- The king's judges then decided what the punishment should be for the guilty. (A bit like the teacher then deciding you have to mop the custard off her neck and pay to have her dress cleaned. Get it?)
- Townspeople took it in turns to act as 'Constable' to question and arrest suspects. (A bit like a classmate having the job of patrolling the school dining-hall to make sure you keep your custard to yourself in future.)

Cruel crimes

'Crime doesn't pay.' That was the message the law wanted to give to people thinking of a spot of murder, treason or thieving. William the Conqueror may have banned executions but they soon returned after his death.

But even executions were all too soon forgotten, so the officers of the law needed a way of reminding the public to behave itself, like . . .

> *Upon London Bridge I saw three or four men's heads stand upon poles. Upon Ludgate Arch the top quarter of a man is set upon a pole. Upon the other side hangeth the bottom quarter with the leg. It is a strange sight to see the hair of the heads fall off or shrivel away while the gristle of the nose is eaten away and the fingers of the hands wrinkle and wither to the bare bones. It is a sight for all young people and a warning to them that they should behave themselves.*

A schoolteacher came up with this jolly piece of writing! He wrote it as an exercise for his pupils to copy out in Latin – and as more than a little hint to his pupils: 'This is what will happen to you if you don't do as you are told!'

Criminal capers

Henry II's laws were really needed by the poor people of England. While kings and barons fought each other, the bullies in the country took the law into their own hands. The Middle Ages were wild and dangerous times. But it wasn't just the poor peasants who turned to crime . . .
1 Robin Hood may have lived in the royal forests of

Sherwood in Nottinghamshire . . . or he may be an invented character and about as real as Donald Duck. But outlaw Sir Gosseline Denville did exist. After wasting his family fortune he became the terror of the north of England. Like most bullies he liked 'soft' targets and often robbed monasteries and convents. In the end he was cornered in Yorkshire by the Sheriff and 600 men. They called on Denville to give himself up. What happened next?

2 The church was no better. The monasteries owned large areas of land and rented it out. Then they employed tough gangs to collect the rent from poor peasant farmers. In 1317 a gang grabbed a traveller on the path to a monastery and held him to ransom for £200. What was unusual about this gang?

3 A Scottish priest sacrificed a man at a black magic ceremony. He had his hands and feet cut off and his eyes put out as a punishment. Kind King David of Scotland took pity on the priest and gave him shelter in his palace. In 1114 the priest thanked the king by murdering his young son – he used the iron fingers of his artificial hands to tear the child apart. David decided to tear the priest apart . . . how?

4 The de Folville brothers had a fine career in theft and ransom. But when Eustace de Folville joined the army to fight for the king he was pardoned of all his crimes.

182

Brother Richard was a priest. A law officer chased rich Richard till the pilfering priest ran into a church and claimed sanctuary. ('No one can touch me while I'm in the church building.') The officer ignored the sanctuary rules, dragged Richard out and beheaded him. How was the officer rewarded for his success?

5 Sir Roger Swynnerton of Staffordshire was accused of murder. There were several witnesses who said they had seen him do it. Sir Roger was set free to return to Swynnerton village where the murder had taken place. What did Sir Roger do?

6 Henry II became fed up with his Archbishop of Canterbury, Thomas à Becket, and said that he wished he were rid of him. Four knights thought they'd do Henry a favour and get rid of Becket for him. They battered Becket to death as he clutched at his altar. Henry was horrified and felt it was his fault. As a punishment he went to the scene of the murder, walked barefoot into the Cathedral and prayed. There were several monks and priests there. How did they complete the punishment of the king?

Answers:

1 Deadly Denville's gang killed 200 before they were finally overcome.

2 The gang members were all monks! But don't be too surprised – in the 15th century there were records of parsons being arrested for poaching, highway robbery and forging coins. They also had a bad name for gambling and drinking in the local taverns. Two priests were arrested in 1453 for beating up an Oxford man – they were helped in the attack by a measly schoolteacher!

3 A wild horse was tied to each arm and leg, then they were sent off in different directions. Your local riding school will probably not allow you to try this on your teacher . . . but in the name of historical research, it's worth asking, I suppose.

WELL, AT LEAST IT'S A GOOD EXERCISE IN PHYSICS

4 The officer had broken sanctuary rules and killed a priest. The officer was punished by being beaten with rods outside all of the churches in the area!

5 The murderer was so upset by the witnesses that he forced them to pay him 50 marks as a punishment for speaking out against him.

6 They stripped him to the waist and took it in turn to give him three to five lashes from each of them. (That's more lashes than you have on your eyes!)

Painful punishments

Henry II tried to make modern laws but the punishments for breaking them were still very old-fashioned and definitely measly.

The Forger
Name — John Stubbs
Crime — He did make copies of the king's coins and used the forged coins to buy food
Punishment — John Stubbs's hand was tied to a block of wood. A meat axe was placed on his wrist and struck with a hammer till the hand was cut off

[Amputation of a hand was a rare punishment but the law was still in force in 1820]

The Thief
Name — Peter of Clarendon
Crime — Felony. He did steal a horse to the value of two shillings
Punishment — The Sheriff of Wiltshire had a pit dug and filled with water which was then blessed by a priest. The thief was thrown in. If he sank he was innocent. Peter of Clarendon floated and was therefore guilty. He was taken out and executed.

[Sheriff Ranulf Glanville of Yorkshire killed 120 men in this way]

The Beggar
Name — Martin of Cheapside
Crime — Begging for money when fit and able for work
Punishment — Three days and three nights in the stocks in the market place, fed only on bread and water. He was then thrown out of the town and ordered not to return

[The kind Tudors reduced this punishment to one day and one night in the stocks in 1504]

185

The Attacker

Name — Thomas of Elderfield

Crime — Fought against George of Northway and did wound him

Punishment — Sentenced to fight a duel with George. He was defeated, and the law demanded that Thomas's eyes be gouged out by George's family. [It is recorded that Thomas was nursed back to health by St Wulfstan. His eyes were miraculously restored]

The Assassin

Name — The Earl of Athol

Crime — Assassinated King James I of Scotland in 1437

Punishment — Taken to the Cross in Edinburgh where he was crowned with a red-hot iron crown and his flesh was nipped off with red-hot pincers.

The Liar

Name — John de Hackford

Crime — In 1364 he announced that 10,000 men were gathering to murder the London councillors. This caused widespread fear and panic. Punishment — He was jailed for a year. Every three months he was taken out, stood in a pillory (or Stretch-neck) with a stone round his neck and a notice "False Liar" pinned to his chest

The Hawk Finder

Name — John of Rivers

Crime — He did find his lordship's hawk on the roof of his house. He failed to report this to his lordship

Punishment — The hawk shall be fed on six ounces of flesh cut from John of Rivers' chest.

> The Scold
> Name — Ann Runcorn
> Crime — She did disgrace her husband by
> scolding him in public, calling him "villain"
> and "rogue".
> Punishment — Ann was fitted with a cage
> over her head called a "brank". A metal rod poked into
> her mouth to hold down her tongue. Ann had to sit on
> a horse facing backwards, and be led through the market
> where people could mock her.
> [A Brank in the town of Shrewsbury was last used in 1846]

Hawking Henry

A hawk was valued more than a peasant by the lords who
owned it. A 14th-century historian told a story about
Henry II's nasty habit – swearing – and how God taught
him a bit of a lesson . . .

> *In the early days of his reign Henry cast off his best falcon
> at a heron. The heron circled higher and higher, but the
> swift hawk had almost overtaken him when Henry cried
> out loud, 'By God's eyes or by God's gorge, that heron
> shall not escape – not even if God himself has decided it!'
> At these words the heron turned and as if by a miracle stuck
> his beak into the falcon's head and dashed out his brains.
> The heron, himself unhurt, threw the dying bird to the
> earth at the very feet of King Henry.*

Wonder why God killed the hawk and not the offensive Henry?

Jolly John

The first Angevins were just like the first Normans. Father (Henry II) fought against sons Richard I, Geoffrey and Henry. But this time the boys had their mother, Eleanor, on their side. (Henry II tamed her treachery by locking her away for 16 years!)

Henry's favourite son was young John. When Henry found that John had joined his three brothers it broke the old king's heart. He died.

Richard took the throne. (His heart was a lion heart so it was harder to break.) Of course, Richard went off Crusading and got himself captured. John looked after the country, spent the royal money and made plans to pinch Richard's throne.

Richard forgave John ('You are just a child,' he said), then very kindly went off to another battle and got himself killed. John was king! But one of the measliest monarchs of the Middle Ages. He liked fine clothes, fine food, fine girlfriends . . . and he enjoyed upsetting people . . .

- John laughed at the long beards and national dress of the Irish princes – the Irish chieftains were upset.
- John married his cousin; the Archbishop of Canterbury objected but John got the Pope to overrule him – the Archbishop of Canterbury was upset.
- John arranged for the murder of his greatest rival, Arthur of Brittany in France – the French king (Philip II) was upset and went to war (though Arthur was too dead to be upset).
- John picked a new Archbishop of Canterbury against

the wishes of the Pope – the Pope was upset.
- John raised huge taxes from the English people and the barons to fight against France; the war went badly and the barons were upset. This, of course, led to . . .

The Magnet Carter

The Barons made John agree to give power back to them and the people; no taxes, no wars and no laws unless the people agreed . . .

Please note that this is utter nonsense of the kind you would only find in a Horrible History. Any boring teacher will tell you that Magna Carta means 'Great Charter' in Latin.

John died after pigging himself on peaches and cider. But the food in the Middle Ages was so bad he could have died just as easily from drinking a glass of water!

Foul food

In the Middle Ages the Church had rules about what you could (or could not) eat. Until the start of the 13th century adults were 'forbidden four-footed flesh-meat'. (Try saying that with a mouthful of mushy peas.) And no one was allowed meat on a Friday – only fish.

The trouble was, people cheated. If they couldn't eat 'four-footed flesh' then they ate large birds. Turkeys hadn't been discovered so they ate birds called bustards. What happened? Bustards became extinct in England!

Fancy a bit of red meat on a Friday? Then eat a beaver. Beavers used their tails for swimming, so they could be called fish . . . couldn't they? (Er . . . no, actually.) What happened? Beavers became extinct in Britain.

And it wasn't only bustards and beavers that had a hard time. A 1393 French recipe book advised eating hedgehog – skinned, cleaned and roasted like a chicken. Of course, catching hedgehogs was harder in those days. You didn't usually find them ready-squashed in the middle of the road. Or perhaps you did!

Tasty treats
It wasn't only turkey that was unknown to the Middle Age munchers. There were no potatoes either. Imagine a world with no chips or crisps!

190

Of course, they had the dreaded cabbage. But forget school-dinner cabbage – pale grey strips of slime flavoured with sweaty socks. Try this recipe for cabbage soup and see if the Middle Ages people had more scrumptious scran than you . . .

Cabbage soup

¶ You need:
- 600g cabbage (leaves cut into strips)
- 225g onions (peeled and chopped small)
- 225g leeks (white part sliced into thin rings)
- half-teaspoon of salt
- quarter teaspoon of coriander
- quarter teaspoon of cinnamon
- quarter teaspoon of sugar
- quarter teaspoon of saffron strands (rather expensive – can be missed out, or use half a teaspoon of turmeric powder)
- 850 ml water
- chicken stock-cube (or vegetable stock-cube if you're a vegetarian)

¶ Method:
1 Boil the water in a saucepan and crumble in the stock cube
2 Stir in the saffron, cinnamon, coriander, salt and sugar
3 Add the sliced cabbage, chopped onion and leek rings to the boiling stock
4 Cover the saucepan and boil gently for 20 minutes
5 Serve with 1cm squares of toast or small strips of fried bacon on top

The only difference in the original recipe was that it said, 'Boil the cabbages all morning'. But cabbages in the Middle Ages were tougher and needed it. Boil modern cabbages all morning and you'll end up with school-dinner green slime.

When it came to sweet dishes the rich people ate all the sugar they could get their teeth on ... until the sugar rotted their teeth, of course. One flavour that was popular then is rare now – the flavour of roses.

Try this rose pudding and see what you think. (Cooks in the Middle Ages didn't have liquidizers, of course, but you might. Cheat a bit and use one if you have. Any greenfly you've failed to wash off the rose petals will be turned into serious hospital cases.)

Rose pudding

You need:
- the petals from a fully opened rose (well washed)
- 4 level tablespoons of cornflour
- 275 ml milk
- 50 caster sugar
- three-quarter teaspoon ground ginger
- three-quarter teaspoon cinnamon
- 575 ml single cream
- pinch of salt.
- 10 dates (stoned and chopped small)
- 1 tablespoon pine-nut kernels (if possible)

Method:

1. Boil the rose petals in water for two minutes
2. Press the petals between kitchen towels under a heavy weight
3. Put the cornflour in a saucepan and slowly add the milk, stirring all the time
4. Put the pan on to heat and warm until the mixture starts to thicken
5. Pour the mixture into a blender, add sugar, cinnamon, ginger and rose petals
6. Blend until smooth (or until the greenfly have a headache)
7. Blend in cream and salt then return the mixture to the saucepan
8. Heat and stir until the mixture is like thick cream
9. Stir in dates and pine-nut kernels and heat for further two minutes
10. Pour into glasses and leave to cool (stirring to stop a skin forming)
11. Eat this straight from the fridge and amaze your parents... just don't tell them that you pinched a prize rose from the garden

Boozing bachelors

In the Middle Ages everyone drank ale. It was safer than drinking the water in some of the filthy large towns.

Special ales were brewed for special occasions and usually *sold* to drinkers (you'd expect to get your drinks free today). So, a man would brew a 'Bride Ale' when he got married. The wedding guests all bought pots of the ale and the money went to the bride.

Imagine going to a wedding today being told, 'Raise your glasses of champagne and drink a toast to the bride – but don't forget to drop a fiver in the best man's hat!' A measly marriage if ever there was one!

Funerals were another popular occasion for a special brew. The corpse often paid for the special ale . . . usually before he died. This was especially popular with drinkers who liked their ale with a bit of body.

The Church became upset by all this drinking and tried to ban it. People enjoyed themselves too much so the Church decided, 'If you can't beat them, join them.' They brewed 'Churchyard Ales' and sold them to raise money for repairs to church buildings!

The Lord of the manor brewed an ale about three times a year; he expected his workers to buy it at a high price. It was a sort of extra tax the workers had to pay. But sometimes the bachelors of the village were given a challenging treat.

They could drink as much of the ale as they wanted, free . . . so long as they stayed on their feet. If they sat down they had to pay.

Foul food facts
1 Butchers were banned from slaughtering animals in the City of London. They'd been in the habit of dumping the guts on the pavement outside the Grey Friars' monastery. A Winchester butcher killed a cow on the pavement outside his shop, while 15th-century Coventry cooks threw chicken guts out of their kitchen windows into the street.
2 Butchers were not allowed to sell meat by candlelight. This was so the customer could see what they were getting! A man was caught trying to sell pork from a dead pig he'd found in a ditch. He was fastened in the pillory and the rotten meat burned under his nose – a common punishment for this sort of fraud.
3 Large towns had takeaway food suppliers selling delicious thrushes (at two for a penny) and tasty hot sheep's feet. They would even deliver cooked food to your home. (Could the sheep's feet maybe deliver themselves . . . simply stroll round to the customer's house?)

4 If you went to a tavern for a mug of ale you could have 'Huffcap', 'Angel's Food', 'Dragon's Milk' or 'Mad Dog Ale' (*that* had a bit of a bite to it). These were probably safer than Eleanor Rummyng's ale – she allowed her hens to

roost over the brewing vats. Their droppings fell into the ale and old Eleanor just stirred them in before she sold it.

5 Drinks could be pretty nasty with lots of 'foreign bodies' floating in them. One 13th-century writer complained that some ale was as thick as soup. 'You didn't drink it, you filtered it through your teeth.' (Of course, King Edward IV had his brother, Clarence, drowned in a barrel of wine in 1478. Now that's what you'd call a foreign body in your drink!)

6 Many towns checked the quality of bread and punished bakers who tried to cheat. Some were found guilty of adding sand to loaves and, in one disgusting case, a loaf contained cobwebs.

7 Housewives often prepared dough then took it to a baker to be cooked. Some bakers had a clever trick. They placed the housewife's dough on the counter. There was a small trapdoor in this counter with a boy underneath. While the baker kept the woman chatting, the boy opened the trapdoor and pinched a fistful of dough. The measly baker made the stolen dough into loaves which he baked and sold. The housewife paid him for baking her loaf and went home with less than she'd brought. (If he was caught then he spent a day in the pillory – there are no records of the boy-thief being caught and punished.)

8 Servants were forbidden to wear hanging sleeves like their masters. This was partly because lords hated their servants to look too grand . . . and partly because long sleeves dropped into the soup as they served it!

9 Henry VIII is famous for his Terrible Tudor feasts but in 1467 there were feasts just as fattening as those. Richard, Earl of Warwick, threw a little party to celebrate his brother becoming Archbishop of York. The 60 cooks prepared 104 oxen, 2,000 pigs, 1,000 sheep and 13,000 sweet dishes. In case this made the feasters thirsty there were 300 large barrels of ale and 100 casks of wine.

10 Peasants ate bacon because it was easy to kill and salt a pig every winter. They ate vegetables because they could grow those themselves. As a result most noblemen would never be seen eating bacon or vegetables!

Mucky manners

Young people had books to teach them table manners. Unfortunately not a lot of young people could read. It may have been better to have had illustrations to help.

DO NOT *clean your nails or your teeth with your eating knife.*[1]

DO NOT *wipe your knife on the tablecloth.*

DO NOT *play with the table cloth or blow your nose on your napkin.*[2]

1. Scratching your head at the table 'as if clawing at a flea' was also impolite.

2. But it was common for people to pick their noses at the table.

DO NOT *dip your bread in the soup.*	
DO NOT *fill your soup spoon too full or blow on your soup.*	
DO NOT *eat noisily or clean your bowl by licking it out.*	
DO NOT *speak while your mouth is full of food.[1]*	
DO NOT *spit over the table but spit on the floor.*	
DO NOT *tear at meat but cut it with a knife first.*	
DO NOT *take the best food for yourself. Share it.[2]*	

1. You could burp at the table... but not too close to someone's face.
2. And you are asked not to steal food from someone else's plate.

Terrible toilets

The Middle Ages were pretty smelly times. Most rubbish ended in the streets. Butchers killed an animal, sold the meat and then threw the guts into the street. The town councils passed the odd law to clean up the streets and London had public conveniences built over the river Fleet to the west of the city.

One writer said that 'each toilet seat is filled with a buttock' so the boatmen sailing underneath had to watch out!

SO FAR THIS WEEK I'VE HIT THREE ROWING BOATS AND A BARGE

And it wasn't only the boatmen who had this problem. Many private toilets took a bit of controlling. The London council took Thomas Wytte and William Hockele to court in 1321 . . .

A jury decided that Ebbgate Lane used to be a right of way for all men until it was closed up by Wytte and Hockele who built toilets. These toilets projected from the walls of the houses so that human filth falls on to the heads of the passers-by.

Not everyone bothered with a toilet. They shared a room with animals and behaved like the animals. Even by 1515 a

Dutchman was complaining about the filthy English homes . . .

The floors are commonly of clay, strewed with rushes under which lies undisturbed an ancient collection of beer, spittle, grease, bones, droppings of animals and men and everything that is nasty.

Of course, careful housewives collected the family urine because it helped with the laundry! They made their own soap by boiling wood ash with scraps of meat fat. The urine was stored until it was really strong and then added to the wash where it acted as a sort of bleach. (Note: If you fancy bleaching your hair then go to the chemist for the bleach. It will cost a bit more but at least you won't smell like a broken toilet.)

Lousy Lancastrians

The last Angevin king was Richard II. He was a poor weak thing and no one was too upset when his cousin Henry had him thrown off the throne in 1399. Henry Lancaster became Henry IV. He had so many lice on his head they reckoned his hair wouldn't grow. He was lousy . . . the first of several lousy Lancastrian kings.

The trouble is his grandson, Henry VI, was another measly weak king. And weak kings were just asking for strong lords to fight for their throne. When Henry VI went mad in 1453 his Lancaster family started scrapping with the York family for power.

Each family had a rose for a badge – a red rose for Lancaster, a white rose for York. After 30 years of bloody battles, Henry 'Red Rose' Tudor defeated Richard 'White Rose' III but, cleverly, married Elizabeth 'White Rose' York. This brought the fighting to an end. Those battles became known as 'The Wars of the Roses'.

The Middle Ages began and ended with important battles . . . and there were several others in between. If those battles had been won by the losers then history would have changed.

201

Bloody battles

Nowadays wars are fought between machines – laser-guided missiles, tanks, submarines, bombs and aeroplanes. A fighting man can kill a million people at the push of a button and never set eyes on one of his victims.

But in the Middle Ages men fought hand to hand – or at least within arrow-shot of the enemy. There was plenty of blood, plenty of cruelty and lots of stupidity.

But in the excitement of a battle it's easy to make mistakes. Winning (or losing) was often decided by simple decisions. How would history have changed if you'd been in command? What would you have done in these famous battles of the measly Middle Ages?

1 Hastings, 14 October, 1066

Armies:

King Harold of England v. Duke William of Normandy. The first major battle in the Norman Conquest.

Battle:

- 9:00 a.m. Harold's English army are sitting on Senlac Hill, tired but happy to defend the place.
- The Normans have three lines of attack – archers, followed by foot-soldiers followed by knights on horseback.
- The first Norman attack fails – the archers are firing uphill and the English catch the arrows easily on their shields.
- The foot-soldiers advance but the English drive them back with spears and stones (but very few archers).
- The Normans turn and stumble back down the hill. Harold turns to you and asks, 'What do we do now?'

What do you tell him?

2 Bannockburn, near Stirling, Scotland, 24 June, 1314

Armies:

Edward II of England v. Robert the Bruce of Scotland. Battle in Scottish war of independence against England.

Battle:

- Robert Bruce's 40,000 Scots are besieging the English in Stirling so Edward marches 60,000 English soldiers to drive them off.
- When the English draw close to Stirling they see the Scots camped on the far side of a swampy stream, the Bannock Burn.
- The Scottish foot-soldiers are armed with long poles with axe heads and spikes on the end – weapons called pikes.
- They group themselves tightly so that charging knights

will face a hedgehog of metal bristles.

- Edward's 2000 knights want to charge at the pikes, but first they have to tear doors off nearby cottages to make a wooden path across the swamp.

What would you advise Edward to do?

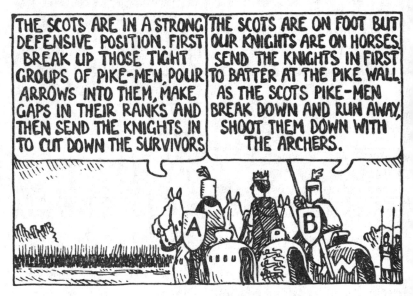

THE SCOTS ARE IN A STRONG DEFENSIVE POSITION. FIRST BREAK UP THOSE TIGHT GROUPS OF PIKE-MEN, POUR ARROWS INTO THEM, MAKE GAPS IN THEIR RANKS AND THEN SEND THE KNIGHTS IN TO CUT DOWN THE SURVIVORS

THE SCOTS ARE ON FOOT BUT OUR KNIGHTS ARE ON HORSES. SEND THE KNIGHTS IN FIRST TO BATTER AT THE PIKE WALL. AS THE SCOTS PIKE-MEN BREAK DOWN AND RUN AWAY, SHOOT THEM DOWN WITH THE ARCHERS.

3 Crécy, Northern France, 26 August, 1346

Armies:

Edward III of England v. Philip VI of France. The first major battle in the Hundred Years War.

Battle:

- Edward's army of 18,000 has less than 4000 armoured knights. He faces Philip's 38,000 men including 12,000 knights.
- The English wait on a small hill. The French have to cross a stream and attack uphill (but this will be no problem for the knights.)

- As the two armies face one another there is a shower of rain. The English take the strings off their longbows and keep them dry. The French archers use crossbows and the soaked string makes them pretty useless.
- The sun comes out and it is straight in the eyes of the French. They can't make out the enemy forces very clearly. They can see that the English archers are at the front.
- Behind the archers the English knights are waiting on foot. The English knights cannot reach their horses in time to fight off the French knights!

What do you advise Philip to do?

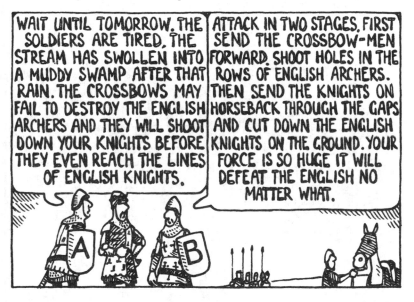

WAIT UNTIL TOMORROW. THE SOLDIERS ARE TIRED, THE STREAM HAS SWOLLEN INTO A MUDDY SWAMP AFTER THAT RAIN. THE CROSSBOWS MAY FAIL TO DESTROY THE ENGLISH ARCHERS AND THEY WILL SHOOT DOWN YOUR KNIGHTS BEFORE THEY EVEN REACH THE LINES OF ENGLISH KNIGHTS.

ATTACK IN TWO STAGES. FIRST SEND THE CROSSBOW-MEN FORWARD. SHOOT HOLES IN THE ROWS OF ENGLISH ARCHERS. THEN SEND THE KNIGHTS ON HORSEBACK THROUGH THE GAPS AND CUT DOWN THE ENGLISH KNIGHTS ON THE GROUND. YOUR FORCE IS SO HUGE IT WILL DEFEAT THE ENGLISH NO MATTER WHAT.

4 Bosworth Field, Leicester, England, 22 August, 1485
Armies:
King Richard III and the Yorkists v. Henry Tudor and the Lancastrians. The final battle in the Wars of the Roses.

Battle:

- Richard has won the race to get his army on higher ground; he has reached the top of Ambion Hill and waits.
- Henry's army had trouble lining up on the rough ground at the foot of the hill.
- Richard could charge at them while they sort themselves out, but he has a couple of problems: a) A third army is waiting nearby under the command of Lord Stanley. Stanley promised to fight for Richard . . . and Stanley promised to fight for Henry Tudor! b) Richard is unsure about one of his own commanders, Northumberland, who is at his back.

What do you advise Richard III to do?

Answers:

1 Hastings Harold follows the advice from soldier 'A' . . . and loses. Once the English leave the hill the Normans turn and attack them on the flat ground. (Some historians believe the 'running away' was just a trick to get the English off the high ground.) It works. Norman archers draw fresh supplies of arrows and fire high in the air. As the English hold their shields over their heads the Norman knights charge them from the front. Harold should have listened to soldier 'B' and stayed where he was. He is wounded with an arrow in the eye then cut down by Norman knights. The Normans will go on to rule England.

2 Bannockburn Edward follows advice from soldier 'B' . . . and loses. The knights feel they are the most important soldiers there and they want the glory of charging at Robert's army first. The archers are hardly used. The knights struggle to cross the swampy ground and then find the Scots have dug pits and traps for the horses. There is no great charge but English knights stumble into Scottish pikes where they are cut down and driven back to drown in the swampy stream. Edward II runs away and his army runs after him. The Scottish people are free of the English.

3 Crécy Philip follows advice 'B' . . . and loses. The crossbow-men fire . . . and are met by deadly showers of arrows from the English longbows. They stumble back . . . and are trampled by their own knights moving forward. The powerful longbows punch holes in the French armour. Horses and knights fall, more horses and knights stumble over them. When a few knights do get through they are surrounded and pulled down by the English knights on foot. Ten thousand French fighters die, and King Philip is wounded by an arrow in the neck but escapes with his life. The English king can claim to be King of France.

4 Bosworth Field Richard follows advice from soldier 'A' . . . and loses. He misses his chance to hit Henry Tudor's army at their weakest. Henry Tudor's men use cannon and arrows to damage Richard on his hilltop. Richard's men come down from their hilltop and fight hand to hand with Henry's men. When Richard calls for Northumberland to move forward with fresh forces, Northumberland refuses. Richard leads a charge personally at Henry Tudor but Stanley decides this is the moment to join the battle – on Henry Tudor's side. Richard is cut down – the second and last English King to die in battle – and Henry Tudor takes the crown. This is the end of the Wars of the Roses. For many historians this is the end of the Middle Ages.

Did you know . . . ?

The Duke of Suffolk had been a loyal servant to Lancastrian king, Henry VI. But when he lost in battle to the French he had to go. Henry didn't want to execute his faithful friend so he sent him off into exile. The Duke of Suffolk set sail from Ipswich but didn't get very far. At Dover his enemies caught

SORRY SUFF, YOU'RE DUFF. I'VE HAD ENOUGH. I KNOW IT'S ROUGH BUT THAT'S JUST TOUGH

up with him, dragged him into a small boat and cut his head off with a rusty sword. (WARNING: Do *not* try this in your local park pond. Cutting someone's head off with a rusty sword could give them a serious case of blood poisoning.)

Sickly singers
Not everyone was horrified by war. Some enjoyed the excitement. Bertrand de Born was a troubadour – a sort of Middle Ages pop-singer. One of his biggest hits was this gory little number . . .

My heart swells up with happiness every time I see
A mighty castle being attacked, its strong walls beaten
   down,
The soldiers on those broken walls being struck down
   to the ground,
While horses of the dead and fallen roam the field at
   random.
And, when battle starts to seethe, let all you noble
   men
Put all your will to breaking heads and arms.
It's better far for you to die in battle than to lose and
   live.
I tell you that my greatest joy is just to hear the
   shouts,
'On! On!' from both sides and the screams of horses
   with no riders,
And the groans of, 'Help me! Help me!' from the
   fallen wounded.
The bliss when I see great and small fall in the ditches
   and the grass

And when I see the corpses pierced clean through by
  shafts of spears!
So, Knights, give up your castles, leave your lands or
  lose your cities,
But my lords, I beg you, never ever give up war.

Woeful women

The Church in the Middle Ages taught that men were better than women. This could have something to do with the fact that the priests were men!

Women were told they had to obey their male relatives till they married, then they had to obey their husbands. Even in the 1990s women can still choose to get married with a promise to 'love, honour and obey' their husbands.

And, if the wife decided to disobey, then the husband was encouraged to beat her. He was told not to do this if he was drunk or in a temper. Just if she 'deserved' it. As an Italian proverb said . . .

A horse, whether good or bad, needs a spur. A woman, whether good or bad, needs a lord and master – and sometimes a stick.

A priest, Robert d'Abrissel, went further when he said:

A woman is a witch, a snake, a plague, a rat, a rash, a poison, a burning flame and an assistant of the Devil.

WHO ME?

211

Do you get the idea that he didn't like women very much? The trouble is men listened to him, believed him and treated women badly because of his wicked words.

Women were told it was sinful to use make-up, to dye their hair or pluck their eyebrows. The priests said this was 'vanity' and women would be punished in Hell. The women did these things anyway.

Then, in the 14th century, priests became worried that men were wearing colourful, fancy clothes and becoming more like those 'snaky, ratty, poisonous' women! And the worst thing a man could do was to be like a woman. That was a sin. So the measly Church started to frown upon . . .

Foul fashions
Fashionable men gave up wearing gowns and started wearing tights. The really fashionable young men wore their tunics so short that a writer complained the tights revealed 'parts of the body that should be hidden'!

The friars, monks and priests had some savage things to say about fancy 14th-century fashions . . .

. . . and the women *did* burn their steeple hats – for a while. When measly monk Tom took himself off, the women went back to wearing their steeple hats which were . . . taller than ever!

In many countries laws were passed in the Middle Ages saying that only nobles could wear fine clothes. Peasants were not to be seen wearing rich clothes – otherwise people would mistake them for someone better!

Most of the laws were there to control women's clothes. Laws were passed to stop women wearing platform shoes, for example. Generally men used any way they could to make sure women 'obeyed' them. As Goodman of Paris told his wife . . .

Copy the behaviour of a dog which loves to obey its master; even if the master whips it, the dog follows, wagging its tail.

But, not surprisingly, women were not always as meek as Mr Goodman would have liked. Women had a difficult a life in the Middle Ages. But some fought back. A few were true . . .

Hooray heroines
Jeanne de Clisson

In 1313 Olivier de Clisson was executed on the orders of Philip the Fair, King of France. His wife, Jeanne, decided he was Philip the Un-fair and decided to get her own back. First she sold off all of her lands to raise money. Jeanne bought three warships; they were painted black and had red sails. Admiral Jeanne began destroying Philip's ships and murdering their crews . . . but she always left two or three alive to carry the story back to the king. After all, that was part of the fun!

Philip died – which could have spoilt Jeanne's fun – but she decided to continue her revenge on his sons as they took the French throne. After 13 bloody years the last son of Philip died and Jeanne retired. It was said that she enjoyed capturing ships with French noblemen on board, then personally chopping off their heads with her axe. (Some women with a fleet may have a fish and chip shop. But when Jeanne caught her enemies on a fishing ship then she would have a fishing-ship chop.)

Her grey ghost still walks the walls of Clisson Castle – don't go there if your name is Philip!

Marcia Ordelaffi

Marcia's husband, Francesco, was not an easy man to live with. In 1358 his son suggested that Francesco should surrender his fortress in Italy. Old Fran didn't like the idea much so he stabbed the lad to death.

The kid killer left wife Marcia in charge of the defence of Cesena a few years later. Sensible Marcia did NOT suggest that they should surrender . . . at least, not until he had gone off to defend another city.

Marcia suspected that one of her councillors was talking to the enemy about a surrender. She had him arrested and beheaded. This was quite a good way to make sure he didn't talk to anyone ever again.

Tough-talking Marcia then talked her way out of the siege and escaped alive with her family.

216

Madame de Montfort

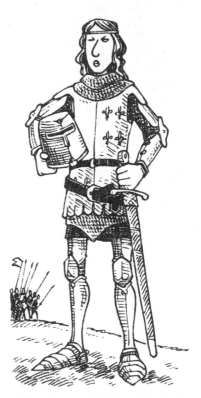

When John de Montfort was captured in a 1341 battle in Brittany, his wife took over the war effort. Apart from raising armies she liked to do a bit of fighting herself. While her town of Hennebont was under siege she rode out in full armour to lead her soldiers. Arrows rained down but she rallied the men. She told the women of Hennebont to cut their skirts short; that way they could run up to the ramparts with stones and pots of boiling tar to pour over the attackers.

When the attackers grew tired Madame de Montfort led a group of knights out of the town through a secret gate. They rode round behind the enemy and destroyed half of the army. The siege was over and Hennebont was saved.

John de Montfort escaped and hurried home to his warrior wife. What did the wimp do next? Help her? Take over as army leader? Give her a thank-you kiss? No! He died! How very inconsiderate.

Madame de Montfort carried on the war for her son. She went mad, was captured by the English and locked away for 30 years till she died.

Jeanne la Pucelle

Jeanne was a French farmer's daughter . . . probably! (Some nutty historians say she was in fact the daughter of the Queen of France!)

Jeanne heard angel voices telling her to lead French soldiers to victory against the invading English. Against all the odds this is what she did.

In spite of being wounded with a crossbow bolt she defeated the English siege of Orléans in 1429. Unfortunately she couldn't defeat France's other enemy, Burgundy. The Burgundians captured Jeanne and very sensibly sold her to the English. The English couldn't execute her as a soldier, so they said she was a witch and burned her at the stake. Her main crime? Wearing men's clothes!

The English lost the war in the end – which served them right for being so mean and measly to this 20-year-old young woman. She became known as Joan of Arc.

Isabella of England

Isabella was the daughter of King Edward III and a useful bargaining tool for old Ed. At three years old she was engaged to Pedro the Cruel of Spain – luckily for Isabella that one fell through! When she was 15, King Ed decided to marry her off to Count Louis de Male. Now King Ed had led the English at the battle of Crécy where Louis's dad had been killed. Louis said, 'No!' to the idea of marrying the English king's daughter.

His people locked him away until he agreed to marry Isabella. After a few months of prison he gave in and he was released from his prison. Louis was still closely guarded, of course, but they said 'he couldn't so much as pee without his guards knowing.' (Charming!) Just before the wedding Louis went out hawking and chased after a heron . . . and didn't stop till he was over the border in France! He'd escaped . . . and Isabella was ditched.

But Isabella was a tough lady. Four years later she promised to marry another young man, Berard d'Albret. Just as she was about to set sail for the wedding in France she changed her mind and went home.

She'd made a monkey out of Berard. Or, rather, she made a monk out of him. Poor Berard was so upset he gave up women altogether and joined a monastery.

Did you know . . . ?

In the 14th century, Emperor Ludwig's daughter was married . . . but it was Ludwig who said, 'I will.' Why? Because his daughter was too young to talk. When she grew up dumb, people said, 'It's God's way of showing that Ludwig shouldn't have married off his baby daughter.' But why did the girl have to suffer? Why didn't God strike Ludwig dumb?

Cheerless children

If women had a hard time then how did children manage? Would you have survived to your present age? Probably not! Look at how the Middle Ages were . . .

Kruel for kids
1 Parents paid little attention to children till they were five or six. After all, they were probably going to die. Only one child in three lived to their first birthday. Only one in ten lived to their tenth. (No one made birthday-cake candles in those days. There wasn't enough business!)
2 Parents of the Middle Ages may have been measly, but at least they were a small improvement on Anglo–Saxon parents. Many of the Anglo–Saxons believed that a child born on a Friday would have a miserable life – so they spared them the unhappiness by killing them when they were born! Others 'tested' the new baby by putting it in a dangerous place – a roof-top or a tree branch. If it cried it was a wimp and was killed – if it laughed it lived. (And if it laughed so hard it fell out of the tree it died anyway!)

221

3 But life was still very tough for children in the Middle Ages. If the plague didn't get you then one of the other Middle Age marauders might! In 1322 Bernard de Irlaunde's baby daughter was playing in her father's shop. A passing pig wandered into the shop, bit the baby on the head and killed her. What a swine!

4 Children from rich families were cared for by nurses. The babies were wrapped in tight bands of cloth so they couldn't move – this was supposed to make their legs grow straight. In fact the lack of use made them weak for a year or two.

5 Peasant children, on the other hand, had no clothes at all until they could walk. Before then they were kept warm by being laid in front of the fire. Curious little crawlers ended up cooked! But even the ones who lay still could have an accident. An old law said . . .

> *If a woman place her infant by the hearth and a man put water in the cauldron and it boileth over, and the child be scalded to death, the woman must be punished for her neglect.*

If there was a law against it then there must have been a lot of cases of it happening. (Notice it's the woman who gets the blame and not the man? But that's another story!)

6 Parents didn't have the Royal Society for the Prevention of Accidents to advise them! They could be very careless about where they left their children. In Canterbury some very young children were left by the river and drowned. In another case an archer was practising his shooting and accidentally shot a child.

GO ON, I DARE YA

7 Worst of all were the beggars who broke their children's limbs so the public would give generously to the twisted, suffering little child!

8 Writers suggested that it was a mistake for parents to be too kind to their children. Children should be respectful to parents. One boy told how he would greet his father with the words . . .

My right reverent and worshipful father, I praise your good fatherhood in the most humble way possible and humbly beg your good fatherhood for your daily blessing.

GOOD BOY. NOW HELP ME WITH THIS CAULDRON OF BOILING WATER

(This may well be a wise thing to say to your own father if you are planning to ask for an increase in pocket money.)

9 Don't laugh, girls. It would have been worse still for you. A book on a girl's behaviour said she mustn't laugh too loud, swear, walk too fast, yawn too wide or jerk her shoulders around. The advice on dealing with troublesome girls went . . .

> *If* your daughters will rebel
> and not bow down low,
> *If* any of them do some wrong
> then do not curse and blow.
> *Just* take a large rod in your
> hand and beat them in a row
> *Until* they cry for mercy and
> until their guilt they know.

This comes from the late-Middle Ages poem, 'How the Good Wife Taught Her Daughter', which was written by . . . a man, of course!

10 Boys who served lords had to stand perfectly still in the

224

castle hall while their masters ate. A 15th–century book said . . .

> ake no seat but be ready to stand until you are told to sit down. Keep your hands and feet still. Do not scratch yourself or lean against a post while your master is present. Bow low and answer your lord when he speaks to you, otherwise stand as still as a stone until he speaks to you.

Sounds a bit like school assemblies today. And, talking about schools . . .

Schools – the good news
- You didn't have to go if you were poor . . . or a girl.
- Most boys only went to school from the ages of 7 to 14.
- There was no homework.
- There were no spelling corrections – you spelled English any way you wanted to.

Schools – the bad news
- You had no break-times – only a short stop for lunch.
- Make a mistake and you were beaten – usually with branches of a birch tree.
- You had to buy your own paper, ink and books – which were very expensive.
- And of course there were 'School Rules' . . .

School rules . . . OK?
Westminster School in the 13th century had the following rules . . .

> ·let them say prayers every morning without shouting
> ·let there be no grinning or chattering or laughing
> ·let them not make fun of another if he does not read or sing well
> ·let them not hit one another secretly
> ·let them not answer rudely if questioned by their elders
> LET THOSE WHO BREAK THESE RULES FEEL THE ROD WITHOUT DELAY!

Not too bad so far? Not much different from your own school, apart from the bit about being hit with a rod!

But if you knew Latin then you *had* to speak it. For each word of English or French that you spoke you received a stroke of the rod. Just imagine, turning to your friend and saying, 'Please can I borrow your book?' would get you six of the best. Measly!

And some of the other rules are odd. But they must have

needed these rules because someone actually did these dreadful deeds . . .

Anyone who has torn to pieces his school mate's bed or hidden the bedclothes or thrown shoes or pillow from corner to corner or thrown the school into disorder shall be severely punished in the morning.

No wonder this boy's 15th-century poem was so popular with pupils. He wrote about being late for school and giving a cheeky reply to his teacher . . .

My master looks like he is mad
'Where have you been, my sorry lad?'
'Milking ducks my mother had!'
It is no wonder that I'm sad.

My master peppered my backside with speed,
It was worse than fennel seed;
He would not stop till it did bleed,
I'm truly sorry for his deed.

I wish my master was a hare,
And all his fat books hound dogs were.
Me, the hunter, I'd not spare
Him. If he died I would not care!

Why was the boy late? You might well ask. Well, school often began at five o'clock in the morning in summer time! Wouldn't you be late?

Schools – the bad news for teachers
- Schoolteachers were not very well paid. Two hungry Huntingdon teachers were arrested for poaching in 1225.
- In 1381 a Suffolk teacher was arrested for riotous behaviour – if he was anything like my teachers then 'riotous behaviour' probably meant laughing out loud at a joke. (A rare event – teachers don't normally understand jokes.)
- In Oxford, England, one teacher's devotion to duty lead to a shocking end. If his pupils had written a diary then it might have looked like this . . .

Dear Diary, today we had a terrible tragedy. Our school teacher Master Dicken, decided to thrash us all with the birch because Peter de Vere left a dead rat on his desk (It was meant to be a gift. Peter's funny like that.) Master Dicken began thrashing the first boy on the register Thomas Abbot and the birch twigs began to split. "Copy out Psalm 34 onto your wax tablets while I collect more birch twigs,"

Master Dicken told us. We went to the
window and watched him march down the
school garden to the river bank. All the
branches hanging over the garden were
dry and brittle. It has been a dry summer.
The really springy hurting branches hung
over the river. We watched, amazed, as he
began to climb the tree and make his way out
to the branches over the river. We counted
as he cut ten, eleven, twelve whippy twigs.
They do say thirteen is an unlucky number.
As he cut number thirteen he lost his hold and
tumbled into the water. His heavy gown soaked
up the water and dragged him down. We
raced out of the classroom and down the
garden to get a better look. Master Dicken
was waving at us. Each time his head came
above the surface he waved. We waved back.
At last his head went under one last time. We
watched for another hour but saw no more of
him. "I think he's in trouble," Peter de Vere
said. "Shall we go for help?" he asked. "Give
it another hour — just to be sure," I told
him.

The teacher died. But death wasn't the only thing faced by teachers. There was worse! Damage to precious school-books! One Middle Ages schoolteacher wrote a letter to a parent complaining of his son's greasy fingerprints and scribbled notes on his books not to mention . . .

In winter it is chilly, his nose runs, and he does not even bother to wipe it until it has dripped and dirtied the book.~

Groovy games you may like to play
At least children in the Middle Ages did have toys – like dolls with their own carriages. The carriages were pulled along by mice. (It's annoying opening a Christmas present today and finding it has dead batteries. Imagine opening one and finding it has dead mice!)

Children played games that are still played today – see-saws, swings, skipping, hide-and-seek, and follow-the-leader.

They also played some very rough games that you may not enjoy so much. Their Blind Man's Buff game was known as Hoodman Blind or Hot Cockles. A child would be 'It' and turn their hood around so it covered their face. They knelt on the ground with their hands behind their back while the others ran past and swiped the hands. If the hooded child guessed who had struck them then the striker became 'It' and so it went on.

Some games were played by adults as well as children. Games like . . .

Raffle

You need:

● three dice
● a score sheet and pen

Rules:

1 Each player takes a turn at rolling all three dice. A player who rolls a 'double' (two ones or two fives and so on) gets a point. BUT . . .

2 If both players roll a double then the highest wins the point. (Double four beats double two, say.)

3 The first player to 10 points is the winner BUT . . .

4 Any player rolling three dice the same wins the whole game with that throw.

Kayles

You need:

● ten skittles (or plastic bottles of the sort used for powdered milk)
● a stick (or a 30 cm ruler)

Rules:

1 Place the skittles in a triangle with the point towards the thrower. The first row has one skittle, row two has two, row three has three and row four has four. (Even you can remember that!) The skittles should be fairly close so that if one falls it will knock over another one.

2 Agree a mark of 2 to 3 metres away from the skittles.

3 Each player throws the stick twice at the skittles.

4 The player who knocks over the most in two throws is the winner.

Note: Another arrangement is to place the skittles in a straight line facing you.

Extra note: In 1477 King Edward IV passed a law banning this game. He probably couldn't stand the thought of poor people enjoying themselves!

Gruesome games you wouldn't want to play

People enjoyed playing ghastly games. Some are still played and have hardly changed in the last 700 years . . .

Camp ball

The game was similar to football. You grabbed the ball and tried to get it into your opponent's goal a few dozen metres or a couple of miles apart. There were any number on each

side and hardly any rules. The trouble was there were no football strips – players wore their normal clothes . . . including knives! In Newcastle-Upon-Tyne in 1280, Henry de Ellington ran into David le Keu. David was wearing a knife at his belt, the knife stabbed Henry in the gut and he died. Deadly David didn't get a red card but hacked Henry probably got a very red shirt.

Stool ball
A milkmaid sat on a three-legged stool. Measly men bowled a ball at her like skittles while she tried to dodge. If they hit her then they got a prize. But beware! The prizes were not gold medals. They were cakes . . . or kisses!

Ice jousting
Ice-skating was popular but the skates were made of animal bones strapped to the feet. The skaters didn't move their feet the way modern skaters do. They pushed

themselves along with poles (like skiers). This harmless sport became deadly when savage skaters charged at each other at speed and used the poles like knights' lances. Lots of broken poles but even more broken bones. Then there was the danger of thin ice.

Archaeologists dug up the skeleton of a woman from the bed of a river. Bone skates were still attached to the skeleton bones of her feet. No prizes for guessing what happened to her.

Snowballing

This popular game was probably played by cavemen. But the people of the Middle Ages had to think of a particularly nasty use for it. They used snowballs to pelt Earl Thomas of Lancaster . . . while he was being taken to his execution!

Middle Ages mind-benders

Pester your parents or torment your teachers with these questions. After all, those wrinklies are a few years nearer to the Middle Ages than you. They have a better chance of getting them right.

1 If you go to a wedding today then you may throw confetti over the bride for luck. In the Middle Ages the guests threw . . .
a) Grains of rice.
b) Tins of rice.
c) Sawdust.

2 Universities were wild places where one rule said . . .
a) It is forbidden to stick a knife in an examiner just because he asks you a hard question.
b) Students who get a question wrong must miss a day's food.
c) Cheeky students must write out 1000 times, 'I will obey.'

3 A miller in the Middle Ages dug clay from the middle of the road to mend his house. What happened next?

a) He was arrested and forced to fill in the hole with stones from the seashore ten miles away.

b) The hole filled with water after a storm and a travelling glove-maker fell in and drowned.

c) The local people took the clay back to the road and the miller's house fell down.

4 Superstitious people in the Middle Ages believed in monsters in far-off lands. One such monster was the Sciapod. He was a one-legged giant. But how did people say the Sciapod shaded himself from the sun?

a) With an umbrella made from the skins of human beings he had eaten.

b) He ripped up an oak tree, rested it on his shoulder and used the branches as a sun shade.

c) He lay on his back, stuck his leg in the air and sheltered under the shadow of his huge foot.

5 The Count of Armagnac argued with his wife over some property. How did he try to persuade her to sign it over?
a) Sent her a wagon-load of flowers, 20 new dresses and a barrel of perfume.
b) Broke a few of her bones and locked her away.
c) Placed a rope around his neck and threatened to jump off the castle roof.

6 In the Middle Ages many lords employed someone called a 'panter'. But what was a panter's job?
a) To look after the pantry in the castle kitchen.
b) To run through the forest (panting) and drive deer out for his lordship to shoot at.
c) To work in the tailor's shop making pants.

7 The peasants' revolt was led by a soldier called Wat Tyler. How did he get the name 'Wat'?
a) His parents christened him 'Wat'.
b) His initials W.A.T. stood for Wilfred Andrew Tyler and 'Wat' became his nickname.
c) Wat was short for Walter.

8 Boys at St Paul's school had to pee into large tubs. Why?
a) Because it was more hygienic.
b) Because the school could sell the urine to local leather workers for softening leather.
c) Because it was too far to the river-side toilets and they would miss lessons.

9 How did monks in the Middle Ages keep the bald patch (tonsure) in the middle of their heads?
a) They polished it with a piece of stone.
b) They singed the hair with a wax taper then dusted the ash off with a leather glove.
c) They pulled the hair out one strand at a time with tweezers.

10 Dick Whittington died in 1423 after twice being mayor of which town?
a) Storytown (because he never really existed).
b) London.
c) Calais.

Answers:

1c) Rice is an Asian crop not grown in England. If any did reach Britain in the Middle Ages then it would be far too precious to waste on a buxom bride! ('Buxom' meant 'obedient' because that's what a Middle Ages woman promised to be.)

2a) Students in Oxford became highwaymen to pay for their classes. The townspeople of Oxford responded by attacking the students – they killed and scalped quite a few! (Punishment c) was still being given to school pupils in the 1970s – but at least they had stopped scalping by then.)

3b) The miller took so much clay that the glove-maker rode into what looked like a puddle but was really deep enough to drown him . . . and his horse!

4c) And if any other Sciapods came along to disturb him then he'd tell them to hop it! (Only joking.)

5b) He was the sort of bully who gets his own way by putting somebody's eye in a sling.

6a) He worked with the ewerer (and if you were a ewerer you were a man in charge of washing the tablecloths and napkins) and with the spit boys (who spitted meat but didn't spit spittle) and with pot boys (who didn't have pot bellies).

7c) Wat Tyler was Walter Tyler. In fact the peasants mightn't have followed him if they'd known they were being led by a Wally.

8b) The school sold the urine and put the money they made towards the school fund. Many modern schools find ways to make money for the school fund. Has your school thought of this one?

9a) They used a type of stone called pumice stone – a sort of volcanic rock that is still sold today. People now use it in the bath to smooth off rough skin on the feet. (WARNING: If you find some in your bathroom, do not practise on your dad.)

10c) Dick Whittington was a real person. Everyone knows the story of Dick and his cat and the bells that said, 'Turn again Whittington and you shall be Lord Mayor of London three times.' BUT not a lot of people know that he was also Mayor of Calais – twice! Which just goes to show, eight out of ten cats (and Calais voters) prefer Whittington!

Rotten religion

People of the Middle Ages were pretty superstitious. They believed in almost anything supernatural, including . . .

Ropey relics
Monasteries collected religious articles. They attracted visitors and were often said to perform miracles. Relics like a tooth of Saint Apollonia – the patron saint of toothache – could cure your tortured tootsie-peg. (Her teeth had been knocked out by the Romans before they burned her.) Hundreds of monasteries had a tooth from her mouth. Big mouth? No, simply another miracle, the monks explained. Henry VI of England collected a ton of them.

Why not start your own collection of saintly relics? Next time you cut your fingernails, save the clippings – that's what one group of measly monks did and said they belonged to St Edmund. Bones make very popular relics. (Your local butcher's shop may be able to help! Many travelling friars used pigs' bones to cheat people.)

Here are just ten 'relics' from churches and monasteries across Europe . . .

● a piece of St Eustace's brain (wonder what it thought about being a relic?)

● wood from the manger in which Jesus was born and the cloth that the baby Jesus was wrapped in
● the coals on which St Lawrence was roasted
● Saint John's handkerchief (complete with Saintly snot)

- one of the stones used to stone St Stephen to death (bloodstained, naturally)
- a piece of the stone on which Jesus stood as he ascended to heaven
- a piece of bread chewed by Jesus
- the head of John the Baptist (Angers and Amiens Cathedrals both had one!)

- the crown of thorns placed on Jesus' head at his crucifixion
- a piece of wood from Jesus' cross (thousands of these).

All right, so I made up the handkerchief, but the others are all genuine relics! Or genuine fakes, but the believers took them seriously. Dead seriously. The monks of Conques pinched a saint's body from another monastery!

One saintly monk was terrified to hear that a monastery was planning to kill him and boil his body down so they could have his bones as relics – he changed his mind about visiting them.

Pay as you pray

In 1303 King Philip of France argued with the Italian Pope Boniface about who people should obey – kings or popes. Philip decided the matter by kidnapping 86-year-old Boniface from Rome. The Pope never recovered from the shock and died.

OH WELL, I SUPPOSE WE CAN STILL SELL HIM IN BITS AS RELICS

The next pope was a Frenchman called Clement. Wise Clement decided to stay in France – after all, the Italians might get their own back and kidnap him if he went to Rome. (There was also a little matter of Clement's girlfriend. He wanted to stay with her in France.)

Once the Pope and his headquarters moved to France they set about cashing in on their power. If you ever become Pope then here are a few measly Middle Ages ways of making money . . .

Religious rip-offs

1 If you commit a sin (like pinching a penny or pinching the bum of the girl in front of you) then the church can

'pardon' you . . . if you pay.

2 If you want to be important in the church (say, a cardinal because they get to wear a red cloak and you think red suits you) then you can have the job . . . if you pay.

3 If a church owns some very holy object (like the toe-nail of a saint or the feather from an angel's wing) then you can have it . . . if you pay.

4 If you give a gift to your local church (maybe money so the church will say prayers after you are dead), the Pope will take a share.

5 The Pope may raise a tax to pay for a Crusade (to fight against the non-Christians in the Holy Land) . . . you fork out, but he won't actually spend it on a Crusade.

6 If you want to be buried in two places at once (your heart in one place and your body in another, like Richard II) then you can have permission . . . if you pay.

7 If you want to marry a close relative (like your dead husband's brother) then you can have permission . . . if you pay.

8 If you are a nun and want to keep two maids (one to do your cleaning and one to do your praying, maybe?) then you can have permission . . . if you pay.

9 If you want to trade with those 'awful' non-Christian chaps from the East (and after all we do want their delicious spices, don't we?) then you can have permission . . . if you pay.

Potty plays

The local craftsmen formed themselves into groups called guilds. Around Easter the guilds came together to produce plays for the people – the masses. These plays were based on Bible stories: Miracle Plays and Mystery plays. That doesn't sound too measly – yet. The guilds performed the plays depending on their own mastery – so they called them mystery plays. Mastery-mystery, geddit?

At first these were performed at the altar of the church – but they became too popular and the churches were full of smelly people. So the plays were moved into the churchyards. But people began trampling on the graves to get a better view. In the end they were taken out of the churches and on to the streets.

The plays were always religious – but that didn't stop them being fun and horribly dangerous! In those days there was no one to give a 'rating' to the plays. Nowadays you know a film is a bit scary if it has a PG (Parental Guidance) rating. In the Middle Ages a lot of the plays were PG – Pretty Gruesome! Which of these horrors could be seen on stage in the Middle Ages?

1 John the Baptist having his head cut off.

2 Jesus being crucified.

3 Jesus rising from the dead and ascending into heaven (or the roof of the stage).

4 The tigers eating the hamsters on Noah's Ark.

5 The donkeys of the Three Wise Men leaving piles of dung droppings on the stage.

6 The Roman Emperor Nero slitting open his mother's stomach.

7 Adam and Eve appearing naked in the garden of Eden.

8 Judas hanging himself from a tree.

In 1326 the people of London turned against the Church because of the taxes it collected. They grabbed a bishop, cut his head off and left his naked body in the street – that was for real; no acting involved!

Batty beliefs
Medieval people believed that in faraway lands there were . . .
- forests so high they touched the clouds
- tribes of people with horns who grow old in seven years
- men with the heads of dogs and six toes
- trees that grow wool

- cyclopeans with one eye and one foot who moved faster than the wind (when told to hop it)
- 100-metre snakes with jewels for eyes.

Eerie eggs.
Got a sickly sister or a plague-spotted pal? Want to know if they'll recover? The doctor would take a hen's egg and write the letters i, so, p, q, x, s, y, s, 9, o on the side. The egg was left in the open air overnight then cracked open in the morning. If there's blood in the egg then call the undertaker!

(Of course this is *nonsense*! But it meant the doctors could say, 'See! They are fated to die. Don't blame me – blame God . . . and here's my bill.')

Miserable monks

Life was unpleasant for peasants. As the Middle Ages went on, some were able to move from the land to the towns which were starting to grow. After the Black Death the Feudal System began to fall apart. Peasants became free to sell their labour or to move.

In towns they could become craftsmen or traders. They weren't tied to the land by the old Feudal System and some grew rich as merchants. But for others the only way out of the measly miserable life on the land was to join the church. Boys and girls as young as seven could be taken on as monks or nuns.

At first the young trainee monks were called novices – a bit like learner drivers in cars today, they weren't allowed to go out on their own. But it was a very hard life . . . even harder than school today! Some of the mini-monks must have had a miserable time . . .

Dear Mum,
  Hope you can get someone in the village to read this to you. The fact is, I want to come home. It's horrible here and I miss your rabbit pies.
  It all starts at 2 in the morning. First prayers. That awful bell wakes us up,

and I have to put on my sandals. I don't have to dress because we sleep in our robes—and they're rotten and itchy. Last night I stumbled into the back of old Brother Benedict. He whipped me with a cane. Have you ever tried praying for two hours with a burning backside?

I got back to bed at 4 and slept two hours—on my face, of course—then that bell's ringing again to call us off to Prime service at 6. Brother Benedict breaks the ice on the water trough and makes me wash. He says it will stop me falling asleep. It just freezes my cheeks. Did you know the Benedictine monks pray at least eight times a day? I asked old Benedict if God wouldn't want us to stop so he could get some sleep. He whipped me—Benedict, that is, not God.

We get breakfast at 7. It's usually porridge. Thin, cold, gritty porridge. Except this morning brother Edward stood on my toe and I cried out. We aren't allowed to make a noise at meals. I was whipped and told I'd eat bread and water for three days. I'd rather have your rabbit pies.

At 8 it's the meeting in the Chapter House — but the novices don't get a word in while the old goats groan on about money and work. It ends with prayers for the dead. But Mum... I don't know anybody that's dead. I sometimes wish I was dead though. Heaven has to be warmer than this place.

After Terce service at 9 we work. It was writing practice in the scriptorium for me. Brother Eamon makes us write on vellum — that's skins taken from the bellies of calves. I wonder why God wants us to do that? This letter's written on the belly of a calf, but I didn't kill it. I can't hold the goose-feather pen in my cold hands. I make smudges and Brother Eamon beats me.

It's High Mass at 11 then off to the fields to work. I had to dig cow muck into the soil. The smell would have made me sick, if I'd had any food in my stomach.

I'm almost glad to get indoors for the None service at 3 then it's lessons till Vespers at 6. I had to sit next to Anthony and I argued with him. He gets beaten as hard as me so I didn't feel too bad. Just hungry.

Compline at 7 and I have bread and water while the other monks eat peas with herbs. That tastes worse than bread and water. Every day, peas and herbs, peas and herbs. Sometimes I imagine I have herbs and peas for a change.

At 8 I have a little time to write this before I go to bed and it starts all over again at 2 tomorrow morning. Just let me come home, Mum, and I promise I'll be the best son you've ever had. I'll walk all the way, I'll pay back the gift that you gave to the monks when they took me in. Just let me come home Mum. I do miss your rabbit pies. Please, Mum.

Your loving son,
Arthur

Mischievous monks

The monks can't all have been saints because rules were written down to say what monks must NOT do. So somebody must have done these terrible things or they wouldn't have had to have the rules! Some of the rules look rather similar to school rules!

A good monk ...

- ☒ will not think too much of his own comfort
- ☒ will not be tempted by rich food
- ☒ will not make a noise in the cloister
- ☒ will not argue with brother monks
- ☒ will not be disorderly in church
- ☒ will not be careless
- ☒ will not disobey senior monks
- ☒ will not become lazy as an old monk
- ☒ will not want his own way
- ☒ will not think of the world outside

Rules for nuns were very similar. How would *you* have survived?

St Roch

People who caught the plague used to call upon the spirit of St Roch for help. Roch caught the plague when he was a young man and went to a wood to die. A dog brought him food and he recovered. When he returned to the town, however, he was suspected of being a spy and thrown into jail where he died. A strange light filled the cell as he died and his captors believed it was a miracle. They decided that if you called for his help then you'd be cured of the plague. On the other hand you may *not* be cured of the plague! This was not St Roch's fault. This was because God decided you had been too wicked.

St Charles

Charles of Blois (in France) was a saintly man. He . . .

- never washed his clothes so he was crawling with lice, put pebbles in his shoes and knotted cords tightly round his body so he suffered pain at all times.
- slept on the straw at the side of his wife's bed.
- made a pilgrimage to a holy place, barefoot in the snow. When his admirers covered the path with blankets he took another road and walked till his feet were frozen and bleeding.

Charles of Blois was a vicious and cruel man. He . . .

- used large catapults to hurl the heads of dead prisoners into an enemy city.
- massacred 2,000 men, women and children when he captured a town called Quimper.

Cruelty alongside saintliness. That pretty well sums up the measly Middle Ages.

Epilogue

Richard III was killed at the Battle of Bosworth Field in 1485. His body was stripped and paraded in public for two days. That was the sort of gruesome spectacle the people of the Middle Ages would have enjoyed.

But things were changing. In England Henry Tudor began a new era – that of the terrible Tudors. The English had been invaded by the Normans, and seen Matilda and Stephen fight a civil war for the crown. The barons had rebelled against King John then gone to war with Henry in another war. Then the country went into a Hundred Years War with France at the same time as it was ravaged by the terrible Black Death. No sooner had the Hundred Years War finished than the vicious Wars of the Roses tore the country apart.

At last Henry Tudor brought a new and wonderful gift to the English people. Peace. And in those peaceful few years the people were able to enjoy life a little more. They became 'civilized'. Life was never quite the same crude, rough, dangerous (and short) thing it had been.

That's why some historians draw the line at the Battle of Bosworth Field and say, 'That was the end of the Middle Ages.' Of course nothing's ever that simple or neat. But things were happening in the rest of the world that meant change was on the way. Just a few years later, in 1492, a bloke called Columbus discovered America. Then Henry Tudor's son, Henry VIII, cut England's links with the Catholic Church and the Pope in Rome.

By the time slimy Stuart king James I united England with her old enemy, Scotland, in 1603, those old days of the measly Middle Ages seemed a world away.

But a clever Frenchman called Voltaire said, 'History never repeats itself . . . humans always do.' The cruelty and stupidity and superstition of the Middle Ages should be a distant nightmare. Yet in the 20th century people can still find ways of making life miserable for others. Bullies with muscles, bullies with money or bullies with power. Just read today's newspapers.

Until they stop we are not really out of the Middle Ages. We're still living in them.

Horrible Histories
The Awesome Egyptians
The Groovy Greeks
The Rotten Romans
The Cut-throat Celts
The Vicious Vikings
The Angry Aztecs
The Measly Middle Ages
The Terrible Tudors
Even More Terrible Tudors
The Slimy Stuarts
The Gorgeous Georgians
The Vile Victorians
The Frightful First World War
The Blitzed Brits

Horrible Histories Specials
Cruel Kings and Mean Queens
Wicked Words
The 20th Century
Dark Knights and Dingy Castles
Bloody Scotland

Also available
Dreadful Diary
Poisonous Postcards
Loathsome Letter-writing Pack

Two books in one
The Terrible Tudors and The Slimy Stuarts
The Groovy Greeks and The Rotten Romans

More Horrible History...

The Frightful First World War
Find out the dire details of the dreadful war that affected *everyone* – from peace-loving protestors (who fought even before the battles began) to the suffering soldiers in the muddy, bloody trenches.

Even More Terrible Tudors
Read on for amazing information about the good times and the gory – from the fabulous fun of the great goose fairs and the harmless horrors of Shakespeare's plays, to the vicious variety of painful punishments and the terrible trickery of the ruthless royal family.

A Horrible Histories Special:

Bloody Scotland
Follow the battling, bravehearted Scots, from the desperate days of the Dark Ages to the terrible 20th century. Discover some sick Scottish torture techniques, and how to terrify a tourist with gory Scottish ghost stories.

Also available:

Dreadful Diary
A foul and fascinating fact for every day of the year. Fill in your own important dates and compare them to the gruesome goings-on of the past with this perpetual diary. Find out what horrible historical event happened on *your* birthday.